# introducing
# INVESTORS
# in PEOPLE

2nd edition

# introducing
# INVESTORS
# in PEOPLE

a manager's guide and workbook

## MARY S McLUSKEY

foreword by SIR TOM FARMER
chairman and chief executive, Kwik Fit

INVESTORS IN PEOPLE

KOGAN
PAGE

First published in 1996
Second edition 1999

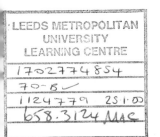

Kogan Page Limited
120 Pentonville Road
London N1 9JN

© Mary S McLuskey 1996, 1999

**British Library Cataloguing in Publication Data**

A CIP record for this book is available from the British Library.

ISBN 0 7494 3103 2

Typeset by Saxon Graphics Ltd, Derby
Printed and bound by Bell & Bain Limited, Glasgow

*This book is dedicated, with love, to Steve.*

# ◀ CONTENTS ▶

# ◀ FOREWORD ▶

The National Standard Investors in People has seen immense growth since it was introduced in the early 1990s. Since that time developments to the Standard have reflected changes in the marketplace and now there is a growing recognition that use of the Investors in People process creates businesses that are strong and fit for the future.

The philosophy of Total Quality Management has gripped many businesses, but my view is that Better Quality Management is a clearer and more understandable way for people to work. Doing something better today than you did it yesterday will help make incremental improvements to the way we work. If all of our people adopt this attitude then businesses everywhere will benefit from continuous improvement.

This book sets out the route through Investors in People and shows how the National Standard links to the European Foundation Quality Model for business excellence (EFQM). Using case studies to illustrate how real businesses have created better working environments, while improving their bottom line, this book offers you the opportunity to get started on the road to continuous improvement.

The case studies are drawn from private and public sector organizations, all of which are recognized Investors in People. The author, Mary McLuskey, has assessed the majority of these organizations. In the spirit of the National Standard, these organizations have agreed to share with you their approach to Investors in People and EFQM, thereby providing you with the opportunity to learn from their experience.

In the final chapter, the author takes a look at the knowledge economy and how learning is impacting on the world of work. The information contained within this chapter reflects the trend in the marketplace towards the learning organization and how the National Standard is adapting to accommodate these changes.

I wish you the very best in your journey towards achieving recognition as an Investor in People. In doing so you will join the ranks of some of the country's most prestigious businesses.

*Sir Tom Farmer, Chief Executive, Kwik Fit*

# ◀ PREFACE TO THE SECOND EDITION ▶

[Since this book was first published the National Standard has been revised in an attempt to simplify the language used and to make it more accessible to all types of business. The contents of my book have been reworked to accommodate the revisions to the Standard. I hope you find the changes helpful and wish you success with your endeavours to achieve recognition as an Investor in People. Before you begin I'll leave you with the following comment:

> *Investors in People does as it claims. For Pieda, it has encouraged us to think much more positively about the needs and talents of all our staff in the context of pursuing our business objectives.*
> Sir Donald MacKay, Chairman of *Pieda* DZT

The National Standard is constantly under review. Currently the government is considering the applicability of the Standard within the context of its Lifelong Learning agenda. The need to enhance competitiveness in the UK has seen a shift from the pursuit of business development as the only means of increasing competitiveness to a broader and more holistic approach. This change in emphasis means that there is recognition that individuals need to be competitive if the marketplace within which they operate is to gain benefit from increased skills and talents. This does not mean that the use of, or indeed the need for, the National Standard is in any way diminished. Indeed, given the development of ideas like University for Industry and Individual Learning Accounts, and the acceptance that skills development is seen as crucial to the social and economic success of the country, the National Standard is more relevant today than it has ever been.

# ◀ ACKNOWLEDGEMENTS ▶

Since this book was first published a number of people have commented on suggested improvements and have provided me with information to improve the contents of this edition. I would like to thank Gerry Farrell for his assistance with the work on linkages to the European Foundation for Quality Management Excellence Model, Fiona Westwood of Westwood Associates for an honest appraisal of the initial copy and Investors in People UK for permission to reproduce the National Standard.

In particular I would like to thank those organizations that have granted permission for the reproduction of material: I believe this is a reflection of the spirit of the National Standard in its widest context. Special thanks to Andy McAlpine, James Coyle, Nicholas Bowd, George Leslie Kerr, Frank Crawford, and Richard Henderson of The Scottish Office for case study material.

# ◀ INTRODUCTION ▶

In 1988 a government White Paper launched the National Training Task Force (NTTF), which was given the responsibility to 'promote to employers the necessity of their investing in the skills of the working population'. From this initiative the National Standard Investors in People was developed and then launched in 1991.

Throughout this book companies that have used the National Standard to focus their business development illustrate the benefits that can be gained. Benefits such as:

**Benefits of the National Standard**

- ninety-eight per cent of postal correspondence dealt with within 28 days, measured against a national target of 90 per cent;
- a crime detection rate of 57 per cent against a national average (in Scotland) of 37 per cent;
- sixty-two per cent increase in turnover with a 60 per cent increase in profitability for a consultancy company;
- a reduction of 27 per cent over three years in the rate of reportable accidents for a major construction company;
- the same company saved 52 per cent of insurance costs for drivers after an extensive training programme;
- labour turnover of 7.8 per cent against an industry average of 13 per cent for a major oil exploration company;

1

- a 31 per cent increase in clients as a result of effective investment in people;
- a 26 per cent increase in customer satisfaction rates for a heavy engineering works.

Several years have passed since the launch, by the CBI and government, of the Investors in People initiative and in this time a number of private and public sector organizations have taken up the challenge of the National Standard. This reflects the growing acceptance in business that focused development of people is a key driver in gaining competitive advantage. This acceptance by business and government has been translated into the ASCETT or NACETT[1] targets. Launched in spring 1994, these targets aim to encourage 70 per cent of organizations employing 200 or more people to commit to or be recognized Investors in People by 2000.

**The Standard creates a focused approach to unlocking human potential**

At present, over 14,000 organizations are recognized against the National Standard and more than 360,000 committed to this path. Although these figures appear small, in real terms they represent approximately 22 per cent of the nation's workforce who are employed by organizations committed to the effective training and development of their staff.

So, what is the National Standard Investors in People? The Standard is a business development tool for unlocking the human potential within your organization. It presents a practical framework for managers to create a culture of wealth generation within individual organizations and ultimately, through the multiplier effect, throughout the country. The Standard is about aligning human resource management to business objectives to create a focused approach to the achievement of those objectives.

Figure 0.1 outlines the process that an organization might use to become an Investor in People and highlights the sections contained within this book that can be used to facilitate the journey.

## How to use this book

The book is designed to explain, in simple language, the National Standard for effective investment in people. It will also assist you to

---

1 Advisory Scottish Council for Training and Targets (ASCETT) is the body established in 1994 whose aim is to promote training and development. The present chairman in Scotland is Professor John Ward. In England this body is known as the National Council for Education and Training (NACETT).

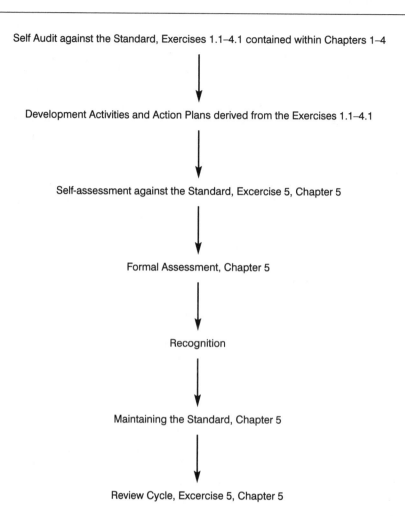

Self Audit against the Standard, Exercises 1.1–4.1 contained within Chapters 1–4

Development Activities and Action Plans derived from the Exercises 1.1–4.1

Self-assessment against the Standard, Excercise 5, Chapter 5

Formal Assessment, Chapter 5

Recognition

Maintaining the Standard, Chapter 5

Review Cycle, Excercise 5, Chapter 5

Beyond the National Standard–EFQM, Chapter 6

**Figure 0.1** *Summary of the process*

identify how you measure up to the Standard and what actions you may need to take to become a recognized Investor in People.

At the end of each chapter a summary of the material covered and a simple exercise are presented. Each exercise is designed to help you to gauge how your organization measures against the Standard and what actions still need to be put in place. By completing each, you will

Logical progres-
sion through the
exercises will
ensure readiness
for assessment

have completed a full diagnosis of your company against the National Standard and will either have produced an Action Plan or will be able to move forward to formal assessment. To embed this material further, illustrations of how this information has been applied in companies are presented. The material used to create these illustrations is based on the information gathered during each company's formal assessment.

The exercises are based on the cumulative experience of assessing Scottish organizations and are designed to eliminate the need for any other assistance – all the questions that you may have at the beginning of the journey towards becoming an Investor in People will be addressed. By working from the first to the last exercise, in a logical manner, you will be sure to have addressed all aspects of the Standard and be ready for assessment.

Finally, in Chapter 5, I have reproduced the storyboards used by two recognized organizations for their assessment. These storyboards are typical of the type that you may wish to produce to facilitate the assessment of your own organization. The companies concerned: *Pieda* plc, the first company illustrated, was recognized as an Investor in People in December 1995. Ethicon Limited was first assessed during June 1993 and recognized as an Investor in People that year. Reassessment took place in 1996 and recognition was retained for a further three years.

## Before we begin

Outlined below is a brief illustration of how one company has recognized the power of effective employee investment and has harnessed the skills of the workforce to best advantage. This illustration shows how a company can make changes to the workplace in a difficult marketplace and gain a competitive advantage through the abilities of the staff they employ.

When I assessed Calor Gas Scotland, the company had already been involved in a number of employee-related programmes that were focused on achieving changes to working practices and to the business operations. A major change management programme had been implemented and explained to staff in some detail. In these circumstances, Calor had achieved something unique. They had implemented major changes with ease and with the full support and commitment of the staff, their communication processes were strong and the fear often associated with change had been managed very effectively. Calor continue to use their communication processes to keep staff abreast of further changes and will, I am sure, continue to be a strong force in the gas market. Calor Gas Scotland were recognized as Investors in People in August 1994.

Their story, part of which is illustrated below, reflects the power of the National Standard and how it can be used by organizations regardless of the pressures of the marketplace.

## Background to the company

A regionalization programme during 1991 to 1993 split the parent group, HSV, into six strategic business units. Calor Gas Scotland is the largest unit and was the subject of the assessment.

Calor Gas Scotland (Calor) had recently undergone a great deal of change. The company had suffered from a round of redundancies, the aim of which was to ensure its continued viability. Calor has a history of strong trade union involvement and through discussion the company has stopped collective bargaining for wages and conditions, although it maintains representation for staff through the TGWU.

Deregulation of the gas industry affected Calor's operations, offering them a market opportunity of which they are taking advantage. Calor Gas is recognized as a market leader in the liquefied petroleum gas (LPG) industry.

Calor Gas Scotland defines its business as:

*The supply, storage and filling in bulk vessels of LPG, the processing of customer orders and the distribution, delivery and periodic maintenance of cylinders. The commissioning of new customers and the provision of commercial and technical support services to all bulk and cylinder customers including the installation and maintenance of pressurized storage at depots and customer locations.*

Calor employs 137 people at three sites: Grangemouth, Aberdeen and Inverness, and has been a registered BN ES ISO9000 (BS5750) organization since July 1992. It is also a supplier to HM The Queen.

Jim Kearney, Calor Scotland's Regional Controller, comments that 'an integral part of our business plan and strategy is to communicate the business objectives to all our employees and the role each individual can contribute towards their achievement. The Investors in People standard has provided the catalyst for improving our business performance and directly reflects the commitment and contribution our people have made to the business. Specific benefits to Calor Gas Scotland include:

- no lost time accidents in 1994;

- business growth by volume and number of customers;
- increased productivity and employee effectiveness;
- improved communications and teamwork;
- enhanced customer service levels;
- focused training and development programmes geared toward business objectives.

These achievements translate into the following business outcomes:

- 55 per cent increase in output per employee;
- 10 per cent reduction in cost per tonne;
- overall business growth of 4 per cent per annum;
- a multidisciplined and skilled workforce;
- an excellent safety record with Lost Time Accident frequency down by 65 per cent;
- 40 per cent reduction in customer complaints.

Raymond Weir, Calor Scotland's then Regional Director, commented that 'as a result of the organizational changes within Calor over the past three years, we recognized that our business objectives could only be achieved by harnessing and developing the skills of our people. Recognizing that our people are our most valuable asset, we are committed to focused development and training for the benefit of the business as well as the individual. We believe by investing in people we are investing in success.'

Calor ensures that all staff are aware of its commitment to train and develop them through a series of documents and by making use of their communication systems. Information is communicated through team briefings, the Quality Policy Statement, Business Objectives and Business Challenge documents. The same systems are used to communicate the aims of the business. Additionally, the company recently introduced a newsletter, *Talkback*, that provides details of any changes in business direction and provides an opportunity for staff to give feedback on any issues that they wish to raise.

The business plan is produced annually and submitted for corporate approval each September. It covers all facets of the business and is translated into key strategic and operational objectives for the coming year. The annual performance plan and previous year's objectives are reviewed monthly at management meetings.

The planning process includes core skills requirements for the following year to ensure that objectives will be achieved, resulting in a company-wide training plan.

Calor make use of job descriptions, personal performance objectives and *Passport to Success* booklets to ensure staff are aware of their contribution to the success of the company. *Passport to Success* restates the company's quality aims and objectives and managers use this document to reinforce the methods through which these will be achieved.

The trade union represented within Calor is the TGWU. Communication with the union is through team briefings and memos. Where necessary, additional detailed information is presented to the union membership to ensure that they are fully informed of the company's aims and how they can support these.

Capital expenditure justification and budget information, which includes relevant information for training and development activity, is included in the business planning process. Included in the current year budget (1994) figures are the costs for the refurbishment of the training room and upgrading of equipment. Other budgeted resources included managers' time and the cost of a training officer.

Planning of all training and development issues is carried out against the business objectives to ensure that these actions will contribute to company success. A company-wide training plan highlights, at a strategic level, those activities that staff will be involved in and is supported by individual action plans where specific training or development needs are not addressed through the company programme. Management meetings are the forum where changes in business direction are discussed and the impact on training and development is reviewed at this time.

Individuals' performance review begins with a training needs analysis at the strategic level. Quarterly appraisals of all staff monitor individual needs and are linked to departmental objectives. All staff have personal and departmental objectives. Staff self-appraise their work prior to their individual meeting with their manager to discuss their past performance and agree new objectives for the next period.

Responsibility for training and developing staff is well defined in the quality manual and in job descriptions for those with this responsibility.

Management competence to train and develop staff is addressed though a series of workshops: 'Core Management Development Skills'. These workshops are run by the company's consultant and are used annually for new managers and managers who require to be updated in these skills.

Training and development plans set out targets and standards required for development actions. Each development activity has a set of well-defined objectives that cover a range of behavioural changes or knowledge-based changes that the delegate is expected to achieve.

Recent examples of development actions included:

- customer care;
- transactional analysis;
- selling skills;
- managing change;
- service standards.

Each of these programmes had a comprehensive set of objectives established prior to delivery.

A variety of external qualifications are used throughout Calor to support staff in their development; examples include:

- RTITB for drivers;
- ImechE for graduate engineers;
- CIMA;
- HNC in Management;
- Diploma in Safety Management.

A comprehensive induction procedure for all new starts and transferees is in operation within Calor. The company makes extensive use of shadowing, mentoring, departmental work instructions and induction checklists to ensure that all aspects of a job are covered over a specified period of time. Self-managed induction is encouraged within Calor to assist individuals to pace their learning to suit their own abilities.

Areas of training and development required to achieve business goals are identified at quarterly and *ad hoc* reviews for all staff. Areas of development are gathered into programmes across the company and individuals are placed on appropriate programmes. Managers who assist individuals in identifying the appropriate method for attaining the required input address any one-off individual needs.

Staff notice boards, *Talkback*, team briefings, *Calor World Magazine*, reviews and informal discussions ensure that all staff are aware of the opportunities open to them.

Job-related development needs are discussed formally at quarterly review meetings and informally on an *ad hoc* basis. Team briefings are also used to discuss issues related to development, and the open style of management ensures that staff are able to approach management as needs arise.

Individual objectives are recorded in training plans and these are used by staff and management to ensure that where a training or development action has been identified, appropriate action takes place.

Involvement of managers in supporting staff to meet their training and development needs can vary from hands-on delivery of instructional training to assisting with the identification of needs and methods of addressing these. Managers spend approximately two hours per week on staff development issues, whether in delivery or discussion of required activity.

The relevance of the development activities of staff to the business is evaluated through key efficiency ratios, volume growth and the business profile showing improved results in key areas.

Training and development actions are evaluated to ensure that objectives are met through a process of review of individual development actions and longer-term monitoring that focuses on the targets set for departments or individuals. Client and staff surveys are used to measure more effectively issues such as job satisfaction, service satisfaction levels and other 'softer' issues.

Outcomes of training and development are evaluated to measure the impact of such activity through course evaluation forms, surveys and post-course debriefs. The costs and benefits of training and development are clearly understood by top management and some of the achievements made through such activity include those listed in the introduction to Calor.

# ◀ CHAPTER 1 ▶

# THE NATIONAL STANDARD: AN OVERVIEW

*Change is the essential process of all human progress*

Science Officer, Mr Spock, Star Ship Enterprise

Investors in People is a simple yet powerful business development tool that, when used as a framework for your human resource practices, will impact upon the success of your business. This Standard is aimed at all employing organizations that wish to make use of their most flexible and potentially most expensive resource: *people*.

**The Standard will revolutionize the culture of your organization**

Unlike other quality standards, Investors in People is a flexible framework that provides the *how* to utilize and profit from the people you employ. It does not give the *what*. So, organizations across the country can adapt the *how* to suit their individual requirements. The Standard is a revolutionary tool that will change the culture of your organization and will empower your staff to deliver business benefits.

In the past, many organizations have not devoted sufficient time to the strategic development of the people they employ. Often business strategies are developed in isolation from this resource although it is the staff who are expected to implement the chosen strategies.

Consequently the human resource function has suffered from lack of access to the top decision makers and to strategy design. The National Standard aims to redress this imbalance by lifting human resource development into its natural home: the strategic arena.

Split into four principles: commitment, planning, action and evaluation, the Standard is divided into a number of indicators or statements that set out the requirements of each principle. In total there are 23 indicators that make up the Standard. Throughout this book reference is made to each of the various parts of the Standard and Appendix 2 shows the whole Standard.

## The nature of commitment

Investors in People requires employers to make a commitment from the top to train and develop all staff to achieve business objectives. This simple statement captures the essence of the Standard. By taking this statement and examining it we can see that an employer should set objectives for the business, communicate these to staff and train and develop those individuals to achieve these objectives. That seems like straightforward common sense. It is! That's why the National Standard is such a powerful tool. There are no mysteries, no hidden difficulties and no reason for not adopting a common-sense approach to developing your business through your people. Making a commitment to invest in your people is the first step towards business success.

**Making a commitment to invest in people is the first step to business success**

## The business plan

The National Standard requires a written business plan for any company intending to be assessed. This document should state the business goals and targets for the period covered by the plan. This is the only piece of written documentation to which the Standard refers; however, as you work through the exercises in this book, you will probably be able to list a number of other documents that you use in your business which can support some or all of the requirements of the Standard. We will revisit the need for documentation later in the book. First let's look at the business plan and which parts of the Standard it can support.

**A company's business plan should state goals and targets**

There are three indicators within the Investors in People National Standard that directly link to the business plan. They provide a key start point in the application of the Standard. The indicators are:

2.1 A written but flexible plan sets out the organization's goals and targets.

2.2 A written plan identifies the organization's training and development needs, and specifies what actions will be taken to meet these needs.

2.4 A written plan identifies the resources that will be used to meet training and development needs.

The three indicators appear in the Planning section of the Standard.

The plan must address each of these three indicators and in doing so will set the framework for a number of others. As the wording of the National Standard suggests, an organization can have separate documents that show the plans for each indicator; however, these plans must link together into a cohesive plan for the whole organization. Figure 1.1 shows a typical business planning process. By using this process we can illustrate how each of these indicators are met using the processes outlined.

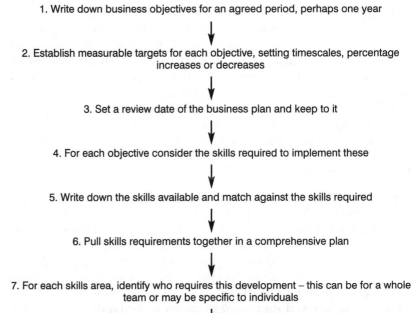

1. Write down business objectives for an agreed period, perhaps one year

2. Establish measurable targets for each objective, setting timescales, percentage increases or decreases

3. Set a review date of the business plan and keep to it

4. For each objective consider the skills required to implement these

5. Write down the skills available and match against the skills required

6. Pull skills requirements together in a comprehensive plan

7. For each skills area, identify who requires this development – this can be for a whole team or may be specific to individuals

8. Identify the costs associated with each development activity

9. Identify the measures that will be used to ensure that skills are gained through the development activity, that is, the method(s) of evaluation

**Figure 1.1** *Business planning process*

### How this applies to the National Standard

In Figure 1.1 the first three points support indicator 2.1. Points 4 to 7 support indicator 2.2, while the remaining points support indicator 2.4.

Each of the steps set out in Figure 1.1 will help with other parts of the Standard. We will, at appropriate points throughout the book, revisit the business planning process.

### The vision

The vision or mission of an organization can be described as the basis from which all decisions within an organization will flow. It will determine the attitudes, policies and practices of the organization, and will assist the decision-making process of all staff during their working day. The vision can influence the strategic direction of the organization and often stems from this.

### How to demonstrate understanding

In the hotel trade, customer satisfaction is of major importance and in many hotels this broad aim takes on strategic importance and will be reinforced in the company's mission and business plan. An example of this is the Sheraton Grand Hotel in Edinburgh, Scotland. Customer satisfaction has a major influence on strategic decisions and on the day-to-day activity within the business. The mission of the organization includes a clear reference to the need for guest satisfaction and this is measured on a regular basis using questionnaires. Staff understand the importance of the guests who use the hotel and this understanding is reinforced through much of the training and development the hotel undertakes. If you ask any of the staff about the hotel's main aims, guest satisfaction will be one of the first responses they give. This understanding has been created through clear communication and support from management and reinforced through training activities.

In the case of Calor Gas Scotland, the business aims and vision of the future were communicated through a series of team briefings from the regional manager and supported by in-house magazines and memos. This approach ensures that the information staff require for their work is provided on a regular basis and in a variety of formats, therefore offering the greatest chance of success in communicating the required message. An additional feature of the processes used by Calor Gas is that staff are able to feed back their responses, verbally and in writing, about any change in the vision, enabling them to influence the decision-making process.

*The importance of two-way communication*

## What people do

Consider for a moment your own job within the organization that employs you, even if you are a sub-contractor, short-term supplier or a casual employee. Now answer these two simple questions: 1) What does your job entail? 2) Do you have all the skills necessary to do this job?

To answer these questions effectively we need a further piece of information, that is, how does your job fit into the whole organization? The answer to these questions will determine three vitally important issues. First, it will help us to understand the contribution that each individual within the organization makes to the business and second it raises the issue of whether this contribution will assist the organization to meet its objectives. The third issue is whether each person is capable of delivering to the organization the contribution that is expected.

**Employees' skills form the basis of a company's human resource strategy**

Within the context of the National Standard, these issues are addressed at the corporate level through the business plan (indicator 2.2), at the individual level through the communication process (indicators 1.3 and 2.3), and through skills development (indicator 3.6). The Standard is set out in Appendix 2 on pages 196–98.

The business plan must address the skills requirement of the whole organization aligned to the strategic direction that it wishes to take. Employers must consider what skills employees will need to deliver the objectives that have been set. Having identified what these needs are, employers must then determine how these needs will be measured and how they will deliver these skills to staff. This information forms the basis of the human resource strategy for the business.

At the individual level, employees must understand their contribution to the business. There are a number of mechanisms that employers can use to help employees understand their role and how that role fits into the organization's strategic plan. Many organizations use job descriptions, team meetings, briefing notes, newsletters or perhaps link communications into performance management systems. The format and level of sophistication that is applied to the communication process will be determined by the culture of the organization. The National Standard requires that employees are clear about what they do and that they understand how this activity fits into the business objectives. It does not prescribe any one method of communication, but it does require communication to take place.

**Well-informed employees make more effective workers**

When individuals know what is expected of them they will be able to work effectively. Clear information will be required for everyone within the business, particularly where changes occur. If everyone in the organization is pulling in the same direction, the business objectives are more likely to be accomplished.

## Demonstrating effective contribution

There are two keys to demonstrating effective contribution. The first is to make clear to each individual what is expected of them. Staff must understand what the job role is and how this links into the wider picture of the whole organization. The second is to measure that contribution on a regular basis and feed this information back to the individual.

*communications.*

The variety of tools and techniques applied within Investor in People companies demonstrate the flexibility of the Standard. The methods used are determined by the organization and operated according to their policies and practices. At the simplest level, verbal communications are acceptable, so long as employees are clear about their role. This approach can work in smaller companies where the need for formal systems is not as great. In larger companies, procedures can become more sophisticated and often written instructions are used as the basis of ensuring that each individual understands their responsibilities and how these should be carried out.

**Targeting and feedback**

Using targets at individual and team level will help with the process of measuring effective contribution and provide employees with a clear picture of how they contribute to the organization. In doing so, a company is beginning to establish the processes that will be used to evaluate the contribution of employees by benchmarking their activities against predetermined standards.

## Trade unions

The National Standard is supported by the trade unions. Those organizations with a union present within the business need to consider the communication processes that are used to ensure that representatives of the union understand the vision of the organization and how they contribute to this.

Where no union exists there is no need, in terms of the National Standard, to introduce one. Where a union does exist, representatives have an important role within the organization's communication process. They add to this process and must, therefore, be able to provide clear information to their members. An example of the process of communication with management, staff and the trade union is described briefly in the following example.

## ILLUSTRATION I

### Foseco (FS) Ltd

### INTRODUCTION TO THE ORGANIZATION

Foseco (FS) Ltd is part of Foseco International Ltd, which forms the major part of the Chemicals Division of Burmah Castrol plc. Foseco (FS) has two manufacturing units in the UK, one in Tamworth, Staffordshire and the other their Carbon Bonded Ceramics plant in Bonnybridge, Stirlingshire.

The Bonnybridge plant was originally an old refractory brickworks. The present technology was introduced in 1980 and Foseco acquired the business in October 1991. Immediately prior to this, Foseco was purchased by Burmah Castrol. The organizational changes made during this time were therefore able to act as the drivers for many changes in the business in subsequent years.

The Bonnybridge site is managed locally and employs 82 full-time staff, 52 of whom are direct labour. They manufacture carbon bonded ceramic pouring tubes for use in the casting of steel which are manufactured on a made-to-order basis for the European steel industry. From four basic shapes the company produces over 600 specific patterns with approximately 200 patterns being manufactured at any one time.

The manufacturing process consists of mixing liquid and granular raw materials in batches to form a mix which is then introduced into moulds and isostatically pressed to form a variety of shapes.

The company had experienced difficulty in achieving performance targets for delivery, quality and reliability. A review of operations identified the main problem as a lack of control of the processes used in the manufacture of the tubes. The company structure was also identified as a barrier to improving the processes. Changes to plant or equipment were unlikely to effect the processes to improve the performance and so the management team took the decision that a radical change to the way specific functions were linked would be the best solution.

At the end of 1993 planning for change began and a series of visits by managers, union representatives and workers to *best practice* companies was undertaken. Team-working conferences were also attended. The result of this activity was the identification of processes that could be implemented: *Kanban* and JIT (Just in Time). One layer of supervisors was removed and a Total Quality Continuous Improvement Through People (CITP) programme was begun.

As a result of these changes the company has made substantial improvements and gained recognition as an Investor in People in 1995.

## Quotations

*We look at what they (staff) do on a weekly and monthly basis. Daily we consider projects and progress against milestones. Bi-monthly we have technical meetings.*

Technical Manager

*The Training Plan for 1995 is now a separate document. It came out of the CITP Steering Group. Previously it was within the body of the business plan . . . We have used training matrices since the beginning of the year. They identify holes and capabilities.*

Quality/Planner

*I was tooling all the time, now I'm pressing and mixing. They (the skills for the job) were built up over time. If the training's done it gets marked up on the training matrix.*

Operator

*I asked about database training . . . I went to Falkirk Tech for nightschool. Its a big help, we used to use big books to record things, now we have a database of stock. . .*

Operator

*There are team meetings and notice boards. Team leaders meet with managers for a team brief, for example, financial information . . . We are 36 per cent more profitable. . .*

Operator

*I have a certificate in Personnel Management from Falkirk Tech. The cost was met by the company.*

Personnel Officer

*We went to Ormidale as part of the selection process for team leaders . . . then we ran a pilot scheme for the teams in the finish end to see how it worked. We then moved onto learn other areas of the process. We meet every eight weeks or so . . .*

Team leader

17

**1.1 The commitment from top management to train and develop employees is communicated effectively throughout the organization.**

Foseco (FS) Limited Carbon Bonded Ceramics intend to build the Bonnybridge plant into a centre of excellence for the development and manufacture of carbon bonded ceramics, formally known as black refractories. To achieve this goal Foseco have adopted a Total Quality Management (TQM) approach.

The principles of TQM have been introduced to Bonnybridge through the development of Continuous Improvement Through People (CITP). The CITP initiative has been the driving force behind a range of developments which have included: creating flexible manufacturing teams, introducing a Just in Time (JIT)/*Kanban* system of manufacture, setting up independent project groups – CITP Teams – to tackle specific quality issues and the introduction of the procedures required to achieve accreditation to ISO9001.

The Training Policy Statement is displayed on the company notice boards and is contained in the *Personnel Manual*; it represents the public commitment of senior management to develop people.

Team Brief 10 was used to launch the CITP initiative, and was used to communicate, as comprehensively as possible, the message that the company was fully committed to developing a skilled, motivated and quality orientated workforce.

**1.2 Employees at all levels are aware of the broad aims or vision of the organization.**

The initial business goals were determined when Foseco (FS) Limited became involved in the Bonnybridge operation; these business goals were set out in a five-year plan titled the Foseco Dyson Limited Business Plan (FDLBP) and published in February 1990. The Mission Statement: 'To become a major profitable supplier of specialist Black Refractory Products to the European Metallurgical Industry', was developed from the business goals by the management team.

The Foseco (FS) Limited Mission Statement was officially launched in February 1994 at Team Brief 10. Team Brief 10 was used as the vehicle to inform the entire workforce of the CITP initiative and to highlight the contribution the workforce would make in achieving the objectives. The message put across was that Foseco are committed to being a profitable, quality-orientated company.

It was recognized that the most effective way to persuade employees of the company's commitment to improvement was to raise the profile of these ideas to the highest possible level. To this end the mission statement and CITP logo were printed onto overall badges, hats and mugs and distributed to the employees.

Management are aware that to motivate people effectively it is necessary to establish trust and provide access to information. Team briefs are given at regular intervals to inform everyone of the company's progress. These team briefs address the pertinent issues of the period, as well as general topics such as quarterly financial results.

Where something that directly effects the entire workforce requires to be addressed, a presentation is given by appropriate members of the management team. Presentations are given to every employee and are generally given to an entire shift, thus ensuring that everyone is present.

**1.3 The organization has considered what employees at all levels will contribute to the success of the organization, and has communicated this effectively to them.**

As part of the introduction of flexible manufacturing teams it was necessary to define the role of each team within the structure; this was set out in the presentation CITP – The Next Step. The teams were split into two groups: production personnel – the people making the product, and production support personnel – every one else. The duties of production support personnel would generally remain unchanged. The duties of the production personnel would require to be clearly defined.

It was decided that traditional job descriptions would act as a barrier to maximum flexibility within the team and flexibility between teams. Flexibility was one of the main reasons for adopting a team-based production system, so a new method of defining production tasks had to be developed. The approach adopted was to develop a matrix that identified all production tasks and a matrix that identified all inspection tasks. Every production and inspection task was associated with a team area and a matrix of the individual tasks displayed in that area.

Team area training matrices are used to represent the different tasks that may be undertaken by the members of a given team. Team members are only allowed to undertake tasks for which they have been trained and are deemed competent; their level of competence is also displayed on the training matrices.

Empowerment meetings were the forum for discussing the introduction of flexible manufacturing teams. The minutes from these meetings describe in some detail the steps to be taken and include some examples of proposed team members.

As strategic members of each team, the duties of Team Leaders had to be considered very carefully. Duties of Team Leaders were detailed in a letter and given to each prospective candidate. The production tasks that Team Leaders are allowed to undertake are detailed on the team area training matrices.

**1.4    Where representative structures exist, communication takes place between management and representatives on the vision of where the organization is going and the contribution employees (and their representatives) will make to its success.**

Cooperation with the unions began with the Memorandum of Agreement, a single union deal which was signed with the General and Municipal Boilermakers (GMB) in June 1992. This deal agreed in principle to the introduction of modern flexible working practices and was part of the foundation for their introduction to the Bonnybridge site.

While investigations were being undertaken into the most suitable form for the flexible manufacturing system, the managers went on several Department of Trade and Industry (DTI) sponsored visits. A conscious decision was made at this time to involve the GMB representatives and as part of the process the shop steward Mr J Carson and the assistant shop steward Mr D Monro were invited to participate.

The GMB have an input to training and development issues through the CITP Steering Group. This is a forum for the discussion of general training issues and is attended by managers, facilitators, consultants and the GMB shop steward.

Wage negotiations are held on a regular basis and recently the first two-year wage deal was agreed between management and unions. There is a conscious effort being made to move towards a single status site, with the introduction of the same terms and conditions of employment for all employees. The CITP Steering Group and wage negotiations are the only formal structures for communicating directly with the unions; however, the company's policy is to keep the unions informed of the 'vision of where the organization is going', forming a mutually beneficial partnership.

## Does a representative structure exist?

In the main, a representative structure is normally taken to be a recognized trade union body. However, some organizations will have internal employee groups such as works councils or informal working parties. Where these exist, the communication processes used will be investigated as part of an assessment, as will the purpose of these groups.

### ILLUSTRATION II

### Oki (UK) Ltd
**BACKGROUND TO THE COMPANY**

Since its establishment in Cumbernauld in 1987, Oki (UK) Ltd (Oki) has grown to become one of the key manufacturing sites in Oki's global strategy. This has largely been as a result of the outstanding performance of a highly motivated and skilled workforce. The company has a total workforce of just under 700 heads (February 1995). The Cumbernauld factory has, since its last assessment, diversified into a broad range of products, including consumables, automotive electronics and new printer products. At the same time the company has coped with increased demand for its ever-improving range of dot-matrix printers.

**1.1 The commitment from top management to train and develop employees is communicated effectively throughout the organization.**

Commitment to train and develop staff is explicit in the managing director's message in the staff handbook, in the company's vision statement and in the education and training policy. A copy of the staff handbook is given to all employees at induction. The company's on-site training school is further evidence of senior-level commitment. This facility was built in 1990 at a cost of over £250,000. Take-up of further education in 1994 exceeded the capacity of the facility, and senior management sanctioned the creation of a further training area. This facility is now located on the fourth floor and is used for delivery of external courses by visiting lecturers.

Commitment is further supported by the participation of various members of the executive and operations management group in, for example, Investors in People Scotland Recognition Panels. Other activities that indicate the level of commitment to and belief in the Investor in People process include: public seminars on Investors in People and other training and development issues; chairmanships of Dunbartonshire and Cumbernauld Education/Business Partnerships; chairmanship of Stirling University's 'Learning in Small Companies' (LISC) project and 'Development of Employer-based Access to Learning' (DEAL); and chairmanship of Scottish Electronics Forum HRD group. Additionally, the company hosts at least one visit per week, often on the topics of training or Investors in People.

Commitment within the company is clearly visible in the high activity levels in training and further education, and the resources allocated to these.

### 1.2 Employees at all levels are aware of the broad aims or vision of the organization.

The vision statement offers the broadest context for the aims of Oki:

Through continuous development of our people and systems, in partnership with our customers and suppliers, to become a world-class manufacturer of high quality products.

This statement was developed in 1990 by a cross-sectional representation of the workforce, and is contained in the staff handbook. Employees meet monthly at the 'Employee of the Month' meeting of the entire workforce, at which company performance against quality, output, efficiency targets and external market position is updated. The company appraisal system ensures that top-level direction is clearly translated into departmental and individual responsibilities.

Over 100 employees took part in cross-sectional workshops in 1993 to consolidate core values for the company's culture. These are:

- Respect all members.
- Promote teamwork.
- Seek improvement.
- Be flexible.
- Keep promises.

Employees are also reminded of company direction when bonuses/ pay reviews take place, as was evidenced by a recent bonus letter.

**1.3    The organization has considered what employees at all levels will contribute to the success of the organization, and has communicated this effectively to them.**

The objectives-setting exercise, which starts with the business plan, is cascaded through the company to identify individual contributions towards organizational success. This communication is further strengthened by regular 'Employee of the Month' meetings, by displaying Departmental Key Results Areas in each department and by morning meetings (*Chokai*) held in each production area. Information about individual and departmental performance, particularly in production areas, is displayed throughout the factory.

**1.4 Where representative structures exist, communication takes place between management and representatives on the vision of where the organization is going and the contribution employees (and their representatives) will make to its success.**

Although not unionized, Oki (UK) Limited has an elected Members Council, which meets monthly with executive management to discuss a range of issues, including company direction and employee contribution. When the new managing director joined in 1994, he made a key-note speech to this group indicating his philosophy for company success. Plans are in place to further strengthen this representative group by provision of a two-day training programme for members' councillors.

These simple illustrations show the processes that can be used to ensure that staff are kept informed of the business direction, their part in its success, the commitment to train and develop each member of staff appropriately and, most importantly, to ensure that the skills of staff are aligned to the business strategy.

Further illustrations, from other recognized companies, will build on the above to demonstrate how these processes affect the success of the business and how this supports the National Standard Investors in People.

**Summary**

The key aspects that you must address from the principle of

**commitment** are: 1) communication to staff (including, if appropriate, trade union representatives) of goals and objectives for the business, the vision or mission, and the attitudes and expectations about the scope of the business; 2) creating a clear understanding among staff about their job role and that they will be provided with training and development to undertake this effectively.

### Exercise 1.1

Exercise 1.1 is presented in two parts. First there is a set of questions that require a simple yes or no answer. By answering these questions you will quickly create a picture of how your business measures against the principle of commitment within the National Standard.

The second part of the exercise uses this information to create an Action Plan to move your business towards recognition as an Investor in People.

From your answers, you can identify those questions to which you responded negatively and begin the process of action planning.

Note: *Remember you will need to answer all questions positively before you can become a recognized Investor in People. The Action Plan is designed to help you towards this goal.*

### Exercise 1.1 – Part 1

|  | Yes/ No | Action required | What action |
|---|---|---|---|
| 1. Have you identified the key skills your employees need to do their jobs? |  |  |  |
| 2. Does your organization make clear to all staff their expectations or vision? |  |  |  |
| 3. Would staff be able to explain to a visitor what the organizational expectations are? |  |  |  |
| 4. Do all of your staff know what they need to do to help the organization meet these expectations? |  |  |  |
| 5. Are they actually doing this? |  |  |  |
| 6. Is there a trade union operating within your business? |  |  |  |

If the answer to question 6 is **No**, you need not answer the remaining questions.

|  | Yes/ No | Action required | What action |
|---|---|---|---|

7. If so, do you communicate with them?
8. Do you know what their objectives are?
9. Do they know what your vision for the future is?
10. Do they know how they support this?

## Exercise 1.1 – Part 2

Each question that you have answered negatively has identified an action point for your organization. You can now create the first part of your Action Plan.

## Action plan

|  | Yes/ No | Action required | What action |
|---|---|---|---|
| 1. Have you identified the key skills your employees need to do their jobs? | No | ✓ | Undertake a skills analysis of staff against business. |
| 2. Does your organization make clear to all staff their expectations or vision? | No | ✓ | Create a vision or mission statement and cascade to all staff. |
| 3. Would staff be able to explain to a visitor what the organizational expectations are? | No | ✓ | Undertake regular checks with staff to ensure they do understand what is expected of them. |

25

# ◄ CHAPTER 2 ►
# PLANNING

*Motivation is what gets you started. Habit is what keeps you going.*

Jim Ryun, athlete

**No business remains static for long periods**

The review and planning process within an organization is central to the Investors in People process and to the success of the business. The flexibility of the National Standard is reflected in the principle of review and it is within this principle that businesses further demonstrate the flexibility of their own planning procedures.

No business remains static for long periods, and consequently a mechanism to ensure that the business remains strategically aligned is essential. This chapter shows how Investors in People companies review their business and plan for the future.

## Strategic resources

From the business plan, the strategic direction will have been established. This strategy will have been broken down into a set of goals and targets that the business wishes to achieve. The next step that has to be considered is the broad development needs of staff who will implement the chosen strategy. All this is considered and captured on paper under the principle of planning at indicators 2.1 and 2.2 (Appendix 2, page 196).

Now the resource implications of these decisions need to be considered. This is crucial to the effective management of the business and effective investment in the training and development function. Clearly defining the resource implications for this function will ensure a focused approach to these activities and will assist in the equally important evaluation of development activities.

**Defining resources and their implications**

Resources can be defined in a number of ways. You may wish to consider, for example, the training and development budget, time spent on these activities, time lost from normal work activities to train and develop, physical resources available such as training rooms and equipment and, of course, people whose time is dedicated to this function.

## Links to the business plan

Chapter 1 made clear that the business plan must include reference to the resources available for the training and development function. In terms of the National Standard, this would be linked to indicator 2.4 (Appendix 2, page 196).

Different organizations will formulate their business plan in different ways. Some will include in one key document all of the information required under the Standard, while others will create business plans that are made up from a series of documents that, taken together, contain all the required information. Remember, the National Standard is about what a business requires to do to invest effectively in people, not about how they should do it.

**Key requirements of a business plan**

The business plan can, therefore, be one document or a series of documents. However, regardless of format, this plan must provide clear information on the strategy of the business, the development needs of the staff to implement the selected strategy and the resources that will be used to support this development.

When considering resources at this point in the business planning process, you should remember all the costs that will be involved and try to capture this information clearly. By doing so you will be able to make better quality decisions about the appropriateness of the identified training and development needs. By committing these resources you are demonstrating your commitment to training and development.

The processes that are used to identify the resources are important. The key to investing in people effectively is to get the best possible return on your investment. So it is essential that an effective mechanism to define resources is used. It is also important that the process used is extended to monitoring the resources set aside. Close monitoring of the resources available and clear definitions of this resource will help to focus the training and development activity on only those actions that will benefit the business. This type of focus is essential for all businesses and will clearly impact on the efficiency of the training and development function.

### Strategic review

### Strategic review of the need to train and develop

**Phasing the training and development strategy**

Having developed a strategic training and development plan for the business, it is important that this is reviewed on a regular basis to ensure that it still matches the business goals. Remember, a strategic plan can change, dependent on the business.

It is unlikely that, having drawn up the training and development strategy, you will deliver this whole programme immediately. Most organizations will take a phased approach to implementation of such activity, spreading the costs over time. In today's rapidly changing environment this makes sense since the business strategy may also change direction depending on market influences. As the business strategy changes, this will impact upon the training and development strategy and also upon the resources available to implement this. If we look at an example of how this might happen in a business, we can see how important it is that an organization monitor its training and development function.

---

**Scottish Widows**

Scottish Widows is a large life assurance and investment company. In common with other businesses in this industry, legislative changes have had a major impact upon business operations. This legislation requires all life assurance companies to 'disclose to prospective clients the amount of commission that will be made on any sale'. Clearly, all sales staff were aware of the commission rates that apply to different products and how to calculate these; however, as this information was not, as a matter of course, passed on to the clients, there was no need to consider how to do this. Scottish Widows needed to consider how this new development would affect their business and how they would equip staff to deal with this new situation.

The business plan was revisited and the appropriate changes made. The strategic training and development plan was then con-

---

sidered in light of these changes and the sales team targeted for a review of the skills that they would need to adapt to the new legislation. Not all of the sales team would require extensive training; some would need skills to be 'topped up', while others would need more in-depth development. The identification of the broad development needed to assist sales staff to cope with the legislative changes was written into the strategic training and development plan. Individual needs were considered during appraisal meetings with line managers.

This example shows how market pressures can affect the direction of a business and clearly illustrates the need for systems that can cope with reviewing the business and the training and development aligned to the chosen strategy.

## The strategic process and how it links to evaluation

Evaluation of the training and development function is considered in some detail in Chapter 4, page 64; however, evaluation is a cyclical process and needs to be considered at various points along this continuum. If we consider for a moment the purpose of evaluating any process or activity, we will discover that what we want to know is its worth or value. In simple terms, did we gain any benefit from the activity or process that we applied?

Training and development should deliver benefits to individuals and to the business: to be sure this happens it is essential to measure those benefits. This is just one step in the evaluation process. Figure 2.1 outlines a simple but effective method that will help to understand the evaluation cycle. The numbers in brackets relate to particular indicators within the National Standard. You can ignore these for the moment as we will return to the specific evaluation indicators of the Standard at a later stage.

**Training and development should be mutually beneficial**

From Figure 2.1, it is clear that by measuring your current position and establishing clear targets for achievement, the evaluation process has begun.

The business plan (indicator 2.1) establishes the goals and targets that you wish to achieve. The strategic training and development plan (indicator 2.2) incorporated into the business plan established the skills needs to achieve these goals and targets, and this plan outlines the resources (indicator 2.4) required to provide staff with these skills.

What is required now is to consider where the business and the individuals within the business are right now. By doing so you establish the

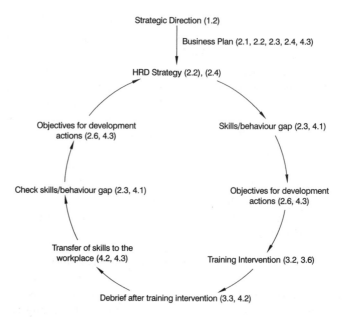

Strategic Direction (1.2)

Business Plan (2.1, 2.2, 2.3, 2.4, 4.3)

HRD Strategy (2.2), (2.4)

Objectives for development actions (2.6, 4.3)

Skills/behaviour gap (2.3, 4.1)

Check skills/behaviour gap (2.3, 4.1)

Objectives for development actions (2.6, 4.3)

Transfer of skills to the workplace (4.2, 4.3)

Training Intervention (3.2, 3.6)

Debrief after training intervention (3.3, 4.2)

**Figure 2.1** *Business planning cycle*

**Establishing a starting point for evaluation**

start point (see Figure 2.2) for evaluating the effectiveness of the training and development function.

For example, a business has established that strategic direction will be based on cost differentiation, and a goal of a 5 per cent increase in the value of sales from all clients within a period of 12 months has been set. It has been decided that this will be achieved through a telesales campaign. An appropriate development activity might be to undertake telephone selling skills training.

If this is delivered in house by an experienced telephone sales person the cost will be reduced. Let's say the cost of training four people in these skills is £3,000. This includes time lost by the experienced staff member from his or her own job, the cost of utilizing the training room, the time spent on training the four members of staff and the resources used to deliver the training.

The objective is to increase the value of sales from the current client base by 5 per cent over a period of 12 months.

The current value of sales is £350,000.

The percentage increase required (5 per cent) is therefore £17,500, which would give a new sales figure of £367,500 by the end of the agreed period.

So, the cost of training the four members of staff is £3,000 and this will generate new sales of £17,500. The benefit to the organization from this one activity is anticipated as £17,500 less the cost of training, giving a payback of £14,500.

This gives a target for increased sales, but to be sure that this has been achieved we need to monitor progress regularly. This can be done in a number of ways: two are given here. At monthly team meetings, actual sales are discussed and noted. These are measured against the targets set. Management meetings also have this information, so business goals are reviewed against actual achievements.

**Monitoring training progress**

The value of the training is clear and continued updating and use of these skills should continue to increase the revenue generated by the sales team. Continued monitoring of sales targets will identify continued benefits and highlight the need for any additional training.

This simple example shows the strategic links from the business planning function to the evaluation of the training and development function.

## Individual review of the need to train and develop

So far we have considered training and development at the strategic level. The question now is: how do the individuals within an organization fit into that strategic process?

Figure 2.2 illustrates a process that can be used both strategically and at individual level; it links closely to Figure 2.1. We will use Figure 2.2 to show how individuals fit into the corporate plan. In doing so, some assumptions are made. The main assumption is that a strategic training needs analysis has been made (Figure 2.1) and that the job holder concerned understands that his or her training and development fits within this analysis.

The start point for each person is a discussion with his or her line manager about the person's present job role and future developments within that role. The job under review is not expected to change for some time, perhaps six months. The discussion revolves around the employee's present capabilities and how these can be improved. During the conversation, the employee cites one or two occasions where he has felt unable to provide the quality of information required by colleagues. This employee, Tom, feels that he is under-utilizing the software package that is installed on his computer and would like to learn how to make better use of what is already available to him.

**An individual's needs may highlight broader company issues**

Tom and his manager discuss the issue for some time, probing why this development is required, what would be gained from undertaking

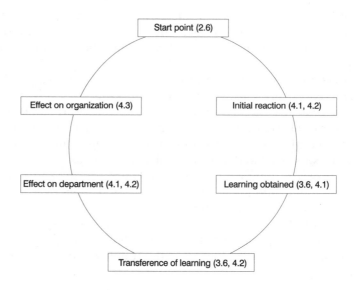

**Figure 2.2** *Process of evaluation*

this activity and how best such development might be delivered. Tom's manager realizes that the problem is not isolated; a recent management meeting highlighted similar problems and the company as a whole is aware that their market position is being threatened by lack of high quality information being made available when required. Indeed, they are so concerned about this that they have written into the business plan an objective of increasing the quality of internal communications and are considering ways in which to achieve this.

**Shadowing**

Through discussion, Tom and his manager are aware that the business as a whole needs to look at this area so Tom's request to further develop his skills in using the software available to him is timely: there is a business need as well as an individual need.

Using the process outlined in Figure 2.2, Tom and his manager capture information about his current skills level, the start point for the development activity.

Next, they consider the appropriate development method(s) and agree when this will be actioned. In this instance, Tom is to shadow a more senior colleague for a period of one week to be shown the different uses of the software package.

To evaluate how effective this activity is, Tom is required to identify his present skills level and to state, as clearly as he is able, what he hopes to achieve by undertaking the shadowing process. Tom's line manager costs this activity in terms of the time that Tom will lose from his normal activities and in the reduced production that will result from the colleague Tom will shadow. He estimates this to be £1,250 based on the cost of both salaries for the week's development activity.

Although this figure at first appears high it is balanced against continued business survival and against recent lost orders worth several times this amount. Management and staff knew that these orders were lost as a result of poor quality information, leading to high levels of customer dissatisfaction and providing an opportunity for competitors to gain advantage.

On completion of his shadowing experience, Tom has a second meeting with his line manager. This is an informal debriefing session that aims to capture Tom's initial reaction (see Figure 2.2) to the development and to attempt to harness some of his newly discovered information. Tom is able to identify several areas of software use he was previously either not aware of or was under-utilizing. Both Tom and his line manager take notes of the meeting and agree to meet again to discuss how he is applying this new knowledge to his job after a period of four weeks.

After the agreed period Tom and his line manager meet and discuss whether he has been able to apply this knowledge to his job. The line manager has also discussed with several other members of staff, who work with Tom, whether there has been an improvement in the quality of his output. Armed with this feedback, Tom and his line manager are able to identify several examples of how the training helped, in terms of speed of delivery and in the quality of information. One colleague is able to show that a new order was successful because the turnaround time for information was able to match that of a competitor and that the quality of this information gave an edge to the sale.

Two clear benefits have been identified and it is clear that Tom's new skills have been transferred to his work. Other benefits are now becoming clear. Tom's position in his department has been enhanced; he is considered more effective and is better regarded by his peers and colleagues. The department is able to rely on the quality of information Tom provides and this has created an added impetus for the sales team to become more proactive. As they do so, sales are improving and this is reflected by increased profit margins over a period of six months.

**The cost-effectiveness of training is well proven**

Review and monitoring timescales will vary depending upon the training and development activity and this example is only meant to illustrate the application of the process outlined in Figure 2.2.

### The individual process and how it links to the business plan

Consider a car and the gears in that car. When driving around a corner, it is normal to drop into second gear. This makes controlling the car easier and alleviates pressure on the engine when it is running at a lower speed. If you attempt to drive around a corner in a higher or lower gear the engine will either race or labour and consequently is not working efficiently. You may take the corner relatively safely, but the engine will have been over-stretched. Your business is like the engine in the car. If the people you employ are over- or under-stretched, you may still make profit, but consider how much more you could make if every single individual worked efficiently.

**Employee efficiency has a cumulative effect**

The individual actions of every employee within your business have a direct effect upon the success of your business. The effects may not always be obvious instantly, but the cumulative effect will eventually tell. Just like the car that is abused by poor technical driving skills, the engine will eventually send a warning and if not rectified, disaster may well ensue. In a car, specific parts of an engine are designed for a particular job. People are not as easy to pigeonhole; however, their role is equally vital to the business of driving the organization in the direction in which it wants to go.

Considering, on a regular basis, how each individual fits into the business is critical to the smooth operation of that business. Figure 4.2 on page 60 shows the business planning process used by Scottish Widows. The process is very sophisticated and reflects the complexity of the company's structure and its size.

### Responsibility and competence

From the information given in the previous section it is clear that individuals have an impact upon others and consequently upon whole organizations. Tom and his manager were able to make a link between his lack of skills in a particular area and the business as a whole. Not all individuals will be able to do this and managers have a responsibility to assist and support their staff in this area.

**The manager's role**

The National Standard requires that managers are competent to train and develop their staff. Organizations will be required to define what they mean by competent managers before they can comply with this statement. Generally, managers should be capable of coaching staff and able to review their performance within their job. Leading from this, managers should also be able to assist staff in setting goals and objectives that are linked to the business plan. How organizations decide to ensure that managers have these skills is entirely their choice.

## What do managers do?

Managers have in the past suffered from a 'bad press'. In Britain the function of management has not always been seen as a separate and viable activity. Developments such as the Management Charter Initiative (MCI) have assisted in defining what the management function is. Within this management standard there are four key functions that managers are expected to perform. These are:

- people;
- finance;
- information;
- operations.

Using this information as a basis to outline management activities, the National Standard is concerned only with the ability to develop people. It is not that the other areas are considered less important, more that all other activities are managed through competent staff.

It is therefore essential that managers are able to develop their staff and to do so must be competent in the appropriate skills. Where managers are new to such a function, it is the responsibility of their line manager and themselves to gain such competence.

The management function within any organization is critical to its success. Without competent managers, the organization is in danger of strategic drift, poor planning, low motivation or staff morale and consequently likely to fail.

Managers may be competent in all the skills highlighted above; however, the National Standard seeks to assess the ability of managers to develop staff. It does not test financial or other technical skills: that is the function of the organization in which they work.

## Setting the standards

Within the Standard, indicator 2.6 states that *'Objectives are set for training and development actions at the organization, team and individual level'*. Evaluation is required at three levels: individual, team and organization. It is, therefore, easy to consider targets and standards at these three levels. If we work in reverse order, it becomes clear how this can be done. At an organization level, the business plan sets the targets that are expected to be achieved over a particular period. The following example illustrates the first step of the progression through the three levels.

**The Scottish Agricultural Organization Society**
## INTRODUCTION TO THE COMPANY

The Scottish Agricultural Organization Society's mission statement is:

*The purpose of SAOS is to create competitive advantage for Scottish farmers and other rural producers, through the support and development of a strong farmer-controlled business sector.*

SAOS encourages cooperation as a means by which farmers can improve their returns from the marketplace and influence the costs of both inputs and production.

SAOS aims to provide the best communication and development services to enable Scottish farmers' cooperatives to reach further and achieve higher performance on behalf of their members.

This statement sets the organizational standard for the service levels that customers can expect and that staff have to deliver. SAOS's aim is to strengthen the profitability of farming and other rural industries in Scotland by supporting and developing cooperation and cooperatively organized businesses.

SAOS achieves its aim by:

- encouraging cooperation by producers in rural Scotland representing the interests and concerns of cooperative business to government;
- contributing to the growth of cooperative business;
- developing and implementing strategies for sectors facing particular difficulty and need;
- designing innovative structures to help the rural economy to adapt to change;
- promoting and pursuing the highest standards of quality and management in rural cooperative business;
- forming partnerships with others responsible for rural business to pursue common objectives;
- publicizing the benefits of and opportunities for cooperation.

This statement sets the targets expected at an organizational level and provides the links into team and individual target and standard setting. Using SAOS to illustrate this process further, we can see how team targets and standards link to the business goals:

| | |
|---|---|
| **Objective – Financial:** | To secure a sustainable ongoing positive revenue account for SAOS (taken from the key objectives). |
| **Result:** | A 20 per cent increase in combined income from all sources. |
| **Objective – Relocation:** | To make the move to Ingliston positively enhance SAOS's achievement of its primary objectives, and its relationships with other industry organizations. |
| **Result:** | Achievements included: move to Ingliston. |

*Excellent forward planning and organization resulted in problem-free, low-cost move and team cohesiveness has been enhanced through working in an open plan environment.*

**Chief Executive**

| | |
|---|---|
| **Objective – Training:** | To progress SAOS's staff training following the intensive needs appraisal in 1991. |
| **Result:** | A comprehensive training plan including several development activities linked to external qualifications. |

Clearly, the setting of targets and standards is central to the process of planning in a successful business. Organizations will be able to establish appropriate targets and standards within their own business goals. The illustration shows how one such organization used the process to set individual and team targets and standards within the context of the whole organization. The process supports many of the practices required within the National Standard and does not sit in isolation. These links will be explained at the end of this chapter in the summary.

## Linking targets and standards to evaluation

From the last section, we can see that setting targets and standards are clearly linked to the evaluation of the business. By putting a stake in the ground and measuring where individuals, teams and the organizations are at present, we can begin the process of evaluation.

**Putting a stake in the ground**

To measure effectively any development actions we first need to know where we stand at the present time. This implies that some kind of systematic process should be used to keep track of developments: whether these actions were appropriate to the organization and the individuals taking part in them. If, for example, an organization has a target of increasing customer satisfaction and wants to improve this, they need to know how satisfied customers are at present.

**The value of customer surveys**

By asking customers about the level of service or quality of the product the organization will know its current standing. Let us assume that such a survey has been undertaken and that the present level of customer satisfaction, in terms of speed of delivery, is 75 per cent. The organization is now able to decide whether this is acceptable or whether an increase is required. If the organization wants to improve this to 90 per cent they then need to decide how to achieve this. In making this decision, they have set a target, that is, a move from 75 to 90 per cent customer satisfaction in speed of delivery. The standard is also set: 90 per cent on-time delivery of products or services.

The organization now has to develop its people to ensure that they will be capable of making this improvement. To measure how effective this development has been, a second survey of the same customers after the development actions will reflect any change. If the survey is carried out a second, third or fourth time, the organization has a set of figures that can be compared against each other to measure the effect of the training or development activity. This comparative analysis can be used to show how the organization evaluates its development activities and to measure the effectiveness of these activities.

## Vocational qualifications

**Vocational awards establish the criteria for many business skills**

Vocational qualifications are standards that have been produced by leaders in industry and education to provide a framework for the development of individuals. These qualifications are assessed either in the workplace or at a centre for education or training. The qualifications are expressed as competencies: statements of what an individual 'must be able to do' prior to gaining an award. There are several awarding bodies that provide a range of qualifications, for example City and Guilds Institute of London, Royal Society of Arts, British Polymer Training Association. The number of awards available is vast, but well worth investigating as these awards establish the criteria for many of the skills used in today's working environment.

Vocational qualifications can be linked to setting targets and standards. There are vocational qualifications in a wide variety of activities. These qualifications can help managers and staff to set clear development actions and, if linked to business goals, will make the process of monitoring progress relatively straightforward.

## ILLUSTRATION

### Danisco Pack, Sheet Feeding (Scotland)
## INTRODUCTION TO THE COMPANY

Danisco Pack, Sheet Feeding (Scotland) is part of the Danisco Group. Formally known as Crown Corrugated (Scotland) Ltd, the company operates as part of the Danisco Group manufacturing division. The company was established in Scotland in 1984 and has two sister companies in Timperley, Cheshire and Merthyr Tydfil, Mid-Glamorgan. The company achieved BS EN ISO 9002 registration in 1987. The Danisco Group is based in Copenhagen and it acquired Crown Corrugated (Scotland) Limited in October 1995.

Danisco Pack, Sheet Feeding (Scotland) meets the requirements of the Investors in People Scotland guidelines on autonomy through the following:

- They have their own business plan and control over this.
- They develop and implement their own training and development plans.
- They have control over their budget and are able to allocate resources to suit their business needs.

In addition, the company has a separate identity and the loyalty of staff to the Larkhall site.

The company is Scotland's only dedicated sheet feeder plant and supplies corrugated sheet board to sheet converters who then print the boxes for their customers. The company has a large number of customers in central Scotland, Ireland and the North of England.

Danisco Pack, Sheet Feeding (Scotland) is the first of the group's companies to be assessed against the National Standard Investors in People and is supported in this endeavour by the group. The Welsh company is currently working towards the National Standard.

### PLANNING: THE EVIDENCE

#### 2.1 A written but flexible plan sets out the organization's goals and targets.

A three-year business plan establishes the goals and targets and the annual budget for the company. This plan is devised by the management team. It is presented to the Group's divisional management team for approval in Spring each year.

The plan contains detailed targets and is supported by the management action plan. This plan contains the broad objectives that form the basis of an annual operating plan. These objectives and production targets are monitored weekly at management team meetings and tracked monthly using statistics. Progress against the plan is communicated to staff at quarterly team meetings.

**2.2 A written plan identifies the organization's training and development needs, and specifies what actions will be taken to meet these needs.**

The training and development plan covers three main areas:

- management development (including supervisors);
- operator training;
- other training needs.

The plan is based on the management action plan and is devised by the management team. The weekly management meetings have training and development as a standard item on the agenda. Progress towards achievement of the plan is monitored at these meetings. An external consultant is currently assisting the company with a business-wide review to identify training needs for the next year.

**2.3 Training and development needs are regularly reviewed against goals and targets at the organization, team and individual level.**

Training and development activities are monitored at weekly management meetings. All training is linked to a specific company objective and targets set for these actions. Statistical information is gathered weekly and reviewed during management meetings. For example, the company set a target of reducing average debtor days from 77 to 72 days and monitors this through the value of credit notes issued.

Two processes are used to review the training and development needs of staff. Weekly paid staff are reviewed by peers on a day-to-day basis and at weekly shift meetings. On a day-to-day basis the quality of each individual's work is checked by the person to whom he or she feeds work in progress. Supervisors monitor work activity and provide support where necessary to resolve problems. Members of the team communicate using hand signals and a series of alarms to halt production at any time where the quality of work in progress is not to the required standards. At the end of each shift a brief meeting is held to 'hand over' to the next shift. These meetings are used to discuss issues related to development needs for staff and these issues are discussed in more detail by supervisors at weekly shift meetings.

All other staff are reviewed using a six-monthly appraisal meeting. These meetings identify training and development needs and review past activity to ensure that the employee skills meet the business requirements.

**2.4 A written plan identifies the resources that will be used to meet training and development needs.**

The resources required to meet the training and development needs of staff are identified in the Training Plan and Budget. These resources include:

- a training room;
- various items of equipment including VCR and television;
- a full-time training supervisor;
- finance for external courses;
- payroll provision for the opportunity cost of training and development activity.

In addition, managers' time is devoted to training and development activities, for example in developing and monitoring the training plan. The training budget for the present financial year is set at £40,000, a substantial increase on last year's budget. This increase is aimed at providing 'Coaching for Results' training for all staff.

**2.5 Responsibility for training and developing employees is clearly identified and understood throughout the organization, starting at the top.**

The general manager has overall responsibility for the training and development of all employees. Day-to-day responsibility is cascaded to the management team and to supervisors.

**2.6 Objectives are set for training and development actions at the organization, team and individual level.**

Pre-briefing discussions are used to ensure that development activities have clear goals and targets set. External courses are discussed and the expected outcomes discussed and recorded. Internal training and development activity follows the same pattern and the company has designed a series of training modules related to operator's work that establish clear standards for training. These modules are being used to supplement training and development received through the industry body responsible for setting industry standards in fibreboard production, the British Fibreboard Packaging Association (BFPA).

**2.7 Where appropriate, training and development objectives are linked to external standards, such as National Vocational Qualifications (NVQs) or Scottish Vocational Qualifications (SVQs) and units.**

BFPA courses are offered to staff twice a year. The training room walls were covered in external certificates from this body and from a number of external training providers. The company is considering the way forward for the accreditation, possibly with SQA, for their training modules and will make a decision on this in the near future.

## Summary

The key aspects that you must address from the principle of **planning** are:

- producing a written business plan which shows the results you wish to achieve for an agreed period of time;
- producing a strategic human resource plan that outlines the training and development needs of staff, aligning these needs to business objectives;
- identifying the resources required to deliver the human resource strategy;
- implementing a strategic review of the human resource strategy to maintain alignment to the business goals and targets;
- implementing a review process for all individuals within the organization;
- communicating clearly to all staff responsibility for training and development;
- expressing clearly the skills required by managers to train and develop staff and implementing an appropriate method of measuring this;
- identifying standards and targets for development actions;
- considering the use of external qualifications or standards for the development of staff.

**Exercise 2.1 – Part 1**

1. Does your organization have a written business plan?
2. Does this plan state clearly the goals and targets you wish to achieve?
3. Does your organization monitor progress towards these goals and targets?
4. Does your organization rethink its goals and objectives in the light of marketplace changes?
5. Have you written down the key skills that your employees will need to implement your business plan?
6. Have you a procedure in place to identify the key skills your employees will need to implement your business plan?
7. Does your organization have a written human resource plan?
8. Does this plan state clearly the resources you will need to achieve the business goals?
9. Does your organization monitor the human resource plan to ensure it is still relevant to the business?
10. Does your organization rethink its human resource plan in the light of marketplace changes?
11. Have you written down the new skills that your employees will need to implement changes to the business plan?
12. Have you a procedure in place to identify the new skills your employees will need to implement changes to your business plan?

| | Yes/ No | Action required | What action |
|---|---|---|---|

13. What process or system do you use to make sure that your employees have these new skills?

14. Does your organization make clear to all staff who is responsible for their training and development?

15. What steps have you taken to ensure that managers are able to train and develop their staff?

16. Do all your staff know why they receive training or development?

17. Are they set goals and targets for development actions?

18. Is there an opportunity for staff to gain formal qualifications during their training?

*If the answer to question 18 is No, you need not answer the remaining questions.*

19. If so, what is the relevance of these qualifications to your business objectives?

20. How do these qualifications assist staff to achieve goals and targets?

## Exercise 2.1 – Part 2

Each question that you have answered negatively has identified an action point for your organization. You can now create the first part of your Action Plan.

## Action Plan

| | Yes/ No | Action required | What action |
|---|---|---|---|
| 1. Does your organization have a written business plan? | No | ✓ | Create a business plan |

| | | Yes/ No | Action required | What action |
|---|---|---|---|---|
| 2. | Does this plan state clearly the goals and targets you wish to achieve? | No | ✓ | Set clear goals and targets for each objective. |
| 3. | Does your organization monitor progress towards the goals and targets? | No | ✓ | Develop a method to measure the achievement of goals and targets. |
| 4. | Does your organization rethink its goals and objectives in the light of marketplace changes? | No | ✓ | Establish a regular timescale to review the business plan. |
| 5. | Have you written down the key skills that your employees will need to implement your business plan? | No | ✓ | Undertake a training needs analysis. |
| 6. | Have you a procedure in place to identify the key skills your employees will need to implement your business plan? | No | ✓ | Establish a process to review the skills of staff. |
| 7. | Does your organization have a written human resource plan? | No | ✓ | Create a plan for the development of your staff. |
| 8. | Does this plan state clearly the resources you will need to achieve the business goals? | No | ✓ | Use this plan to estimate the cost of this development. |

|  | Yes/ No | Action required | What action |
|---|---|---|---|
| 9. Does your organization monitor the human resource plan to ensure it is still relevant to the business? | No | ✓ | Build into the business planning cycle a review of this plan. |
| 10. Does your organization rethink its human resource plan in the light of marketplace changes? |  |  |  |

# ◀ CHAPTER 3 ▶

# TAKING ACTION

*If you only look at what is, you might never attain what could be.*

Unknown

## Getting the best out of the new start

Induction is a powerful tool that every employer has the ability to make use of. By ensuring that new employees are effectively introduced into the organization, an employer provides the messages and philosophy that they wish their employees to adopt during their employment. Perceptions shape our behaviour and form the basis of our reality. What is reality to one person is not the same to another. Induction can shape the perceptions of new employees and so frame their sense of reality. This might appear very simplistic; however, it is in fact quite profound. Induction will begin the process of employees establishing their judgements about an organization and the values it holds. The values of the organization need to be communicated effectively and as early as possible. If this does not happen, the new employees will form their own perceptions about the organization and these may well be in conflict with the true values of that organization. Perception for many is reality, so it is essential to shape these

**Induction can shape the perceptions of new employees: first impressions count**

perceptions as soon as possible to ensure that the employees are able to frame their reality around the ground rules or values that the organization operates: first impressions count.

**Induction is a process, not a one-off event**

Induction can take many forms and will vary depending upon the type of individual and the job that he or she is expected to perform. What is clear from working with organizations that use induction is that the value of this tool is of major importance in making new employees effective quickly. The best companies see induction as a process and not as a one-off event.

**Induction should begin as soon as possible after an employee starts**

When people start a new job, they will need to know more about the organization they have joined than they will have been able to learn from job adverts or from interviews. They will also need to know in detail the specific function they will perform while employed by the organization. The induction or introduction of new employees is crucial to ensure that they are familiar with their responsibilities, duties and the way in which these are expected to be carried out. A general overview of the organization's approach to its business will provide the context in which they will work. The timescale and the level of information provided is for each organization to decide; however, it is essential that induction takes place and at as early a juncture as possible.

**Using checklists**

Many organizations use checklists to ensure that all relevant information has been covered with each new employee and that this information has been recorded. Using such an approach will help the new employee and the organization to identify which pieces of information have been covered and which are still outstanding.

Checklists can be very basic, covering statutory and employment requirements, or they can be more sophisticated and cover all aspects of the organization: job details, performance measures and systems to support these, communications systems and all other relevant information that new employees may need to find their way around the organization and its systems.

Where staff are already employed but change their job function within the organization it is essential that their new duties are made clear and that they are introduced to their new job role and responsibilities.

## The power of effective induction

**Effective induction saves money**

Many organizations that have reconsidered how they introduce new staff to their jobs have discovered that effective induction can have an extremely beneficial effect on the new employee and on the business. Staff are able to fit into the routine of work more quickly; they are able to perform effectively sooner than those not given induction training.

Staff who are properly introduced to the organization are more likely to stay with their employer and contribute more effectively.

Consider the previous statement and the power of an effective induction begins to become clear. Where staff have effective induction training they will become cost-effective employees and so save the business money in doing so. A simple example will help to illustrate this point.

*cost*

---

**Royal Scottish Assurance plc**

**INTRODUCTION TO THE COMPANY**

Royal Scottish Assurance plc (Royal Scottish) is a Royal Bank of Scotland company and a member of the Bank's Marketing Group. Royal Scottish is a dynamic and progressive life company that offers a comprehensive portfolio of life assurance, health insurance, savings, investments and pension products.

The process used by Royal Scottish Assurance involves a comprehensive induction programme, which is spread over a two-week period, for all staff. Shadowing of colleagues is also used extensively to ensure staff are introduced effectively to their jobs. This shadowing process is not restricted to the induction period and complements the systems used to train and develop staff. Where staff are transferred into other departments, specialist training is provided to support them in their new role. Personal development folders and associated key result areas are updated to reflect their new role.

A good induction process is particularly important where an organization uses short-term, casual or sub-contract staff.

---

## The right skills at the right time

Once an individual has been introduced to the workplace and to the job function, it is crucial that, if the employee is to continue to perform effectively, he or she is provided with the skills to do so. This means that an analysis of the employee's abilities against the requirements of the job should be undertaken to highlight any areas of the job in which the employee will need to be trained or developed. This type of analysis should take place at the start of a new job, whether it is for a new start, transferee or promotee, and should continue throughout the employee's working life with the organization. In undertaking this kind of analysis an employer ensures that staff are capable of delivering the kind of service required of them and that staff are clear that where they have a skills shortfall this will be remedied.

**Use analysis to establish an employee's potential**

49

**The importance of timing**

Any training or development activity needs to be delivered at the right time, that is, at a time when the individual who is learning this new skill or behaviour will be able to practise and make use of this as soon as possible. Take, for example, a new manager. This person has responsibilities that include appraising the work of staff. This is a new skill that the manager requires to learn. Rather than provide appraisal training several weeks or months in advance, the employer provides this training a few weeks before the manager undertakes the new role. The training is reinforced by shadowing a colleague and the manager is supported in this new task by a superior or peer.

The training is put to good use since it is timely, has been observed and has been practised all within a short period. If the next time the manager has to use these new skills is some time in the future, a refresher course may be appropriate.

## Providing opportunities for employees to develop in line with the business

Staff need not always take up development opportunities; however, they must be aware of these and be able to make use of such opportunities as are available, regardless of their position in the organization. Within the National Standard, indicator 3.4 (Appendix 2, page 197) examines the methods that an organization employs to ensure that staff have such opportunities communicated to them and the use they make of this information.

It is easy to forget that all individuals who are employed by an organization will have their own opinion about how they want to be developed, if at all. There should be in place a mechanism that enables individuals to discuss this issue and to have an input to their own development.

**Opportunities for discussion**

Organizations will choose the methods that are appropriate to their culture and style. Some organizations will discuss opportunities for development during team meetings, at individual appraisals, through electronic mail, newsletters and notice boards. Whatever method is chosen, staff must be clear that the opportunities presented relate to their development as individuals and to the organization.

If the organization takes a strategic view of training and development (if they wish to become Investors in People, then they must), only relevant opportunities should be made available to staff. The human resource strategy, discussed in Chapter 1, is specifically aimed at ensuring that relevant training and development activity is undertaken.

Relating training and development needs to an individual's job helps to focus discussions and help management and staff to ensure that any development agreed will benefit the individual and the organization. Looking at individuals' jobs and where they fit into the rest of the organization can assist in focusing on why difficulties are encountered, or highlight ways to improve effective systems and help to identify ways in moving forward.

*Focused thinking*

## Making it happen

How does an organization make sure that staff are informed about opportunities, are able to participate in their own development and are provided with the skills they need to do their jobs at the time of starting that job and throughout their time with the organization? There are two key activities that will ensure this can happen.

The first is good communication and the second is the ongoing review of staff performance in the workplace. Effective communication is the key to ensuring that staff are aware of what is required of them. Measuring the effectiveness of the communication process can provide an organization with a clear picture of the differences between staff and organizational objectives.

**Evaluating the effectiveness of communication processes**

Communication audits can reveal whether the messages sent out from the top of the organization have become distorted as they are passed down through the ranks. Often messages are either ignored or are not sufficiently clear for staff to act upon them effectively. A communication audit is one way of evaluating the effectiveness of the communication process.

The second method of ensuring staff are effective is to monitor their work activity. Managers can assist staff by expressing clear objectives and by reviewing these objectives. Staff are then able to conduct their work knowing that they are working to the goals they are expected to achieve. So, where managers ensure that staff have clear objectives and that these are properly monitored, it is only a small step to identifying those areas that are causing an individual difficulty. It is these areas of difficulty that create the need for training and development. To be sure that such a training or development need does exist, managers should revisit the objectives they have been set and establish whether these are still valid. Focusing on business objectives and on key skills is a means of ensuring relevant training.

This then places emphasis on focused training and development. The word 'objectives' is crucial. It implies that objectives for training and development have been set and we know that these should

**Individual objectives must also reflect business goals**

reflect the business goals. By setting objectives for development actions, it is possible to measure the effectiveness of such activity: it is possible to measure any shift in behaviour, attitude, work rate or effectiveness.

## After the rhetoric: taking action

**Using pre-course forms**

When a course of action has been agreed to train or develop an individual, it should take place. The only circumstances where this would not happen are when the employee leaves or changes jobs within the organization or where business goals change sufficiently to affect any decisions made. By agreeing with a member of staff that he or she requires to have some kind of development, you have set up an expectation that this will take place. Not only that, you have identified a need to improve skills, or conversely, you have identified a deficiency. Prior to the training or development activity taking place, staff and line managers should check that clear objectives have been set and that these link to either a personal, team or business goal. A simple but very effective mechanism to ensure that this happens is to have some pre-course/activity discussion and, where the style of the organization permits, to record the content of this discussion. Many companies now use pre-course forms to capture this information. The style of this document will be determined by the company and the individuals using it. The pre-training form requires each activity to be linked to a business goal and to state clearly the expected outcome of the activity. This process maintains the focus of training on business success and ensures that staff are aware of the reasons for and expectations of any such activity.

---

### AC Henderson
#### INTRODUCTION TO THE COMPANY

AC Henderson is a service company operating in the industrial, marine and catering markets. Formed in 1961 by Alex Henderson, the company is now managed by Susan Henderson and is limited by guarantee.

As part of the processes used to support staff AC Henderson use pre-training forms to establish clear targets and standards for each training or development activity. These forms also identify the appropriate method of and timescale for evaluation. The company maintains a training record system to monitor all activities.

Additionally, pre-and post-training forms are used to track training and development results.

This simple but effective tool enables the company to be sure that the development of staff is linked to business objectives and that the development activity is relevant to the individual's job.

## How managers support staff

'Manager' is a broad term used here to describe any individual who has responsibility for people within the organization. This key role requires active participation on the part of the manager to assist staff to identify needs, to train or develop them as appropriate or to provide them with the means of obtaining the training and development they require.

Often staff are clear that it is necessary for them to be given additional training or support to enable them to do their jobs better. Managers should encourage and foster such a dialogue with their staff. In many organizations the support that managers provide for their staff will cover a wide range of activities. For example, managers will be involved in induction training, performance reviews, team briefings, delivering training and coaching staff on a day-to-day basis. All of these activities are considered support in terms of the National Standard. The level of activity and the type of activity will be determined by the organization.

**Ranges of support activity**

*action.*

## The manager's role in making it happen

Managers support staff in a number of ways. Each organization will take a different approach to supporting staff; however, there are some basic methods that most organizations will use to ensure that managers are providing their staff with the assistance they need to do their jobs properly. These were referred to in the section above.

Managers' responsibility in supporting staff should be determined by the company through policies and practices. In many companies where job descriptions are used, these documents make clear what support managers should give to their staff. Each company will determine the level of activity and how this should be applied. If a company is an accredited BSENISO9000/BS5750 organization, then this information is likely to be captured within the documentation used to support this quality standard.

**Types of management support should be contained in company documentation**

**ILLUSTRATION**

**Search Consultancy Ltd**

**INTRODUCTION TO THE COMPANY**

Search Consultancy Ltd (Search) specializes in the recruitment and selection of executives and professionals within the UK and overseas. Search is Scotland's largest independent recruitment and selection consultancy and has offices in Glasgow, Edinburgh and Dunfermline.

Established in 1987, Search has sustained growth of approximately 70 per cent year on year and now ranks among the top 20 companies in Scotland for growth.

Search employs 70 staff who operate a range of recruitment, selection, advertising and personnel management services for the following areas: accountancy, financial services, legal, technical/engineering, personnel, sales and marketing, language, computing, medical, industrial, construction and secretarial.

**ACTION: THE EVIDENCE**

**3.1 All new employees are introduced effectively to the organization and all employees new to a job are given the training and development they need to do that job.**

A standard induction programme is undertaken by all new employees. This programme covers company policies, Health and Safety at Work, statutory regulations and all other aspects of their employment. A second induction activity focuses on formal training that covers all aspects of the new employee's job. A formal presentation, where new staff are given copies of the staff handbook and task books, completes the induction process. Individuals who transfer or are promoted are coached or shadow colleagues as part of an informal process.

**3.2 Managers are effective in carrying out their responsibilities for training and developing employees.**

Managers' effectiveness has been defined by the company as: the ability to appraise staff, interviewing and recruitment skills, motivation, the identification of training needs, setting performance measures, communications skills, leadership skills and dealing with problem employees. A major training and development programme to address these skills has been under way for some time. Managers' effectiveness is assessed in these areas through the appraisal system.

**3.3 Managers are actively involved in supporting employees to meet their training and development needs.**

Managers are jointly responsible for the training, development and review of their staff to ensure continuous improvement in performance. Managers frequently attend training activities with staff to show support and to refresh themselves in particular skills. Coaching, mentoring and advising roles are adopted by Search managers as part of their normal activities. Managers also conduct company-wide training and development activities and deliver specialist, on-the-job and task book training.

**3.4 All employees are made aware of the training and development opportunities open to them.**

Opportunities for staff are communicated through the appraisal system, annual presentations to staff, at induction, during weekly meetings and through documentation such as the staff handbook, task books and the training and development policy. The company newsletter supplements these systems by informing staff of other types of opportunity that arise throughout the year.

**3.5 All employees are encouraged to help identify and meet their job-related training and development needs.**

Pre-and post-development activity forms assist staff in contributing to the identification of their training needs. The appraisal system promotes individual input and staff are encouraged to discuss their own ideas for development with their line manager whenever they wish.

**3.6 Action takes place to meet the training and development needs of individuals, teams and the organization.**

Task books, weekly training needs analysis and monthly managers' meetings are all used to monitor the skills levels of staff and to ensure that, where a gap is identified, it is acted on. Training records are kept for all staff. The training budget reflects the level of training and development activity in Search.

## Summary

The key aspects that you must address from the principle of **action** are:

- introducing new and transferring employees to their jobs and to the organization;
- ensuring that staff have the skills required to do their jobs;
- communicating opportunities for development to staff;
- assisting individuals to identify their own development needs;
- delivering training and development that is relevant to the organization and to individuals' needs;
- ensuring that managers provide staff with the appropriate level of support in the training and development process.

### Exercise 3.1 – Part 1

|  | Yes/ No | Action required | What action |
|---|---|---|---|
| 1. Does your organization have an induction procedure? | | | |
| 2. Does this procedure cover all aspects of an employee's role within the organization? | | | |
| 3. Does your organization have a training policy? | | | |
| 4. Does this policy cover all employees? | | | |
| 5. Are employees aware of the opportunities open to them? | | | |
| 6. Are staff able to request training or development to support them in their jobs? | | | |
| 7. Does your organization record the training and development activities that employees undertake? | | | |
| 8. Are managers active in their support of their staff? | | | |

**Exercise 3.1 – Part 2**

|  | | Yes/ No | Action required | What action |
|---|---|---|---|---|
| 1. | Does your organization have an induction procedure? | No | ✓ | Create an induction pro-gramme. |
| 2. | Does this procedure cover all aspects of an employee's role within the organization? | No | ✓ | Ensure that pro-gramme is adaptable to suit all types of jobs. |
| 3. | Does your organization have a training policy? | No | ✓ | Create a training policy. |

## ◄ CHAPTER 4 ►

# DID WE GET IT RIGHT?

*It is wise to keep in mind that no success or failure is necessarily final.*

Unknown

### Going back to basics: the business plan revisited

**The National Standard aims to ensure that company objectives relate to the business plan**

Remember the written business plan discussed in Chapter 1? In drawing up the business plan a number of broad aims were set for the organization. This document sets out the objectives that the organization hoped to achieve over a specified period.

The evaluation section of the National Standard aims to assist organizations in measuring whether these objectives were achieved. It does this by addressing a number of key issues. The focus of the National Standard is to ensure that individuals within the organization are capable of delivering the objectives that are required of them, and that these objectives relate specifically to the business plan. Figures 4.1 and 4.2 show how a company can use the processes of evaluation to develop their business and to plan for the future.

**Evaluation – the key issues**

So, what are the key issues that the National Standard addresses under the principle of evaluation? There are three levels of evaluation that an organization is expected to undertake:

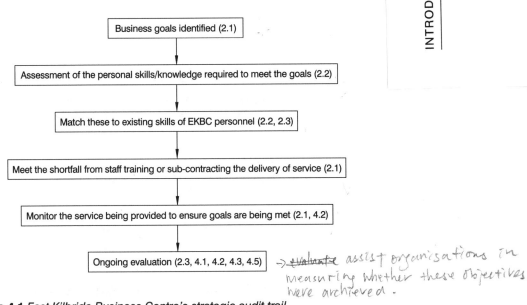

→ evaluate assist organisations in measuring whether these objectives have achieved.

**Figure 4.1** *East Kilbride Business Centre's strategic audit trail*

1. The organization is expected to measure the effect of training and development at an individual level, that is, what individual employees have achieved as a result of any training and development activity undertaken.
2. The organization must consider the impact such activity has had on teams. At this level you may also consider actual team development activities to show what benefits have been gained.
3. The organizational level. At this level companies are expected to show how the training and development of their staff has impacted on the business.

Evaluation (see Figure 4.3) creates the opportunity for organizations to recognize the input of individuals, teams and organizational objectives. It provides a clear focus for the whole organization to realize the value of individual contributions to the success of the business and ensures that each individual can see how he or she plays a part in that success. Like putting the pieces of a jigsaw together, an organization can show each individual has a role to play and that this role has a direct effect on the other members of the organization.

The National Standard provides a simple method to assist you in determining the results of any training and development activity that

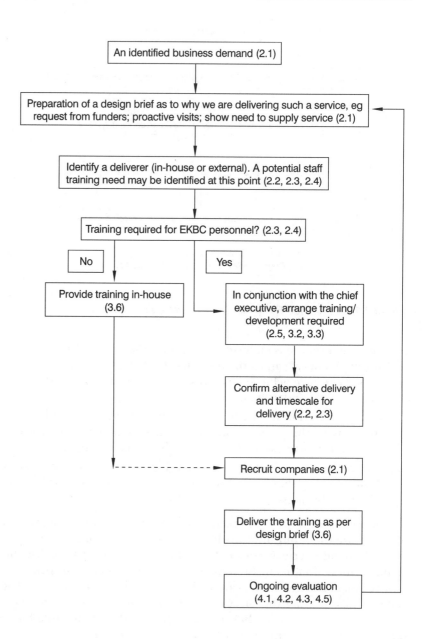

**Figure 4.2** *East Kilbride Business Centre's strategic planning process*

has taken place within your organization. Under the Planning principle, indicator 2.6 (page 197) requires that development activities are clearly expressed in terms of targets and standards. The process of setting such targets and standards should be considered as putting a stake in the ground: identifying the start point from which the organization or individual will move. By identifying clearly what a development activity is expected to change you are expressing the anticipated outcome of that event. In doing so you are beginning the process of evaluation. Using this technique for all training and development activity provides clear parameters in which each activity can be conducted and sets up measures to be evaluated at the end of the process. The diagram in Figure 4.3 shows the effect of triple loop evaluation. The process draws on the triple loop learning theory of Joop Swieringa and Andre Wierdsma.

**Triple loop learning**

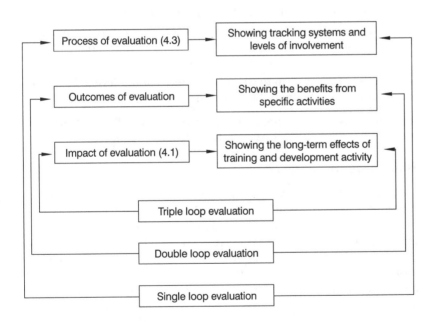

**Figure 4.3** *Triple loop evaluation*

The processes used to evaluate the contribution made by training and development to the success of the business should consider the immediate impact of such an activity, the longer-term effects this activity has had and how effective the processes used are in capturing this information.

**The process of evaluation is simplified if clear objectives for training and development are established**

When beginning the process of evaluation it may help to consider the following levels:

- What were the immediate reactions of trainees to the training? What did they think was relevant, and what were their opinions of the timing, the style of delivery and the content?
- What was learned during the training, that is, what new information or skills have been gained, and does this learning reflect what was expected from the training activity?
- Has the training been transferred to the job? Consider the behaviour of the trainee in the workplace and look at what has changed; for example, has quality improved, or is productivity higher?
- What differences have been made at a team or departmental level as a result of the training received? Are there changes in the team/department? If so, try to measure them.
- Finally, you may wish to consider organizational-level evaluation by looking at profitability figures or increases in new business.

Remember, by establishing clear objectives and targets for training and development the process of evaluation becomes simpler.

### What have we achieved?

**Measurement of achievements must be an ongoing process**

Measuring what has been achieved through development activity is an ongoing process. One-off events can have an immediate impact at any or all of the three levels that the Standard requires to be measured. However, it is equally important to recognize that, in terms of development, individuals and organizations learn at different speeds. To monitor effectively what has been achieved many organizations will take measurements at different times during and after development activities. The planned introduction of development activities will assist in identifying when it is best to measure the outcome or impact of such activity. Clearly, the timing of such measures will change the results. It is not in question that changes over time will occur in the behaviours and learning of individuals, teams or organizations. This is not a reason for not capturing results. Indeed, in terms of the National Standard, changes over time are clear indicators that the company is consistently measuring the training and development activity and its effect on the business.

In considering what has been achieved, it is essential first to consider what we intended achieving. This leads us back to establishing the targets and standards expected from development activities. For example, if the business plan states that the company wishes to increase its customer base by 5 per cent over the next 12 months and that the method employed will be increased selling skills for the sales team, then we have established broad targets for the development activity. To make this more specific, individuals need to know their current level of business activity and what can be reasonably expected of them as a result of the training activity. From here we can set targets for the training activity and move broad objectives into specific targets for the individuals who will participate in the activity.

Let us assume that the sales team is made up of five people. Three of these individuals are able to achieve the expected results at present, while the remaining two struggle to achieve their sales figures. Looking at the team, their line manager considers how best to make the 5 per cent increase in the customer base. She decides to give the whole team selling skills training, focusing on closing the sale as this has proved to be the most difficult area of work for most of the staff. The training will be delivered at morning team meetings in 30-minute blocks over a period of four weeks. The objectives of the activity are:

- to demonstrate the skills required to introduce the company's products effectively;
- to develop the language or phraseology that will assist individuals to introduce these products to customers and to develop the ability to use this language in a relaxed and normal manner;
- to identify the difficulties that individuals have in closing sales and find solutions to these barriers;
- to reinforce product knowledge in terms of their uses and their limitations;
- to develop a customer-oriented approach to selling;
- to develop an effective method to introduce the company's products to new customers.

Each of these objectives is agreed as relevant to the team's training and all five members of the team participate in the training sessions.

At the first session, members of the team have been asked to identify their current number of clients and to establish how many new

**Setting targets**

**Team objectives**

**Comparing weekly statistics**

customers they need to meet the 5 per cent target. An open discussion about the problems associated with this increase results in setting the objectives outlined above. All the team have different concerns but agreed that by participating in each session, they will be able to pass on to each other techniques and tips that they use to gain customers' confidence and loyalty.

The training sessions are held each morning and at the beginning of each new session staff are encouraged to state how the previous day's activity was affected by the training given. This information is recorded by the team's manager. Weekly statistics are used as a normal business monitoring process and the results of the team are compared against the previous week's activity. This helps the manager to check that the training is having the desired effect. After the whole programme has been delivered, the sales team targets are compared against previous month's activity and against the same month in the previous year. These comparisons show the outcomes of training activity very clearly and the day-to-day evaluation of the training sessions help to measure the impact on an ongoing basis. These two processes provided valuable evaluation of the activity.

**Shadowing**

Further debriefing meetings are held with each member of the team and two members asked for additional training. This was agreed and a shadowing event is developed whereby the two most experienced members of the sales team take the two 'trainees' on a number of sales visits. At the end of each session the 'trainee' discusses what has been learned and how they will make use of this information. To ensure that this exercise is of value, the experienced member of the team shadows the 'trainee' on one visit. A debriefing meeting is again held to enable the experienced member to point out to the 'trainee' what, if anything, they would have handled differently. They also point out good practices that were seen and further developments that the 'trainee' might consider for the future. Again, sales statistics monitor the value of this exercise and the debriefing sessions are used to record any changes in behaviour that have occurred.

## Evaluating the impact of the training and development activity

The principle of evaluation in the National Standard outlines the processes required to ensure the relevance, to measure impact and to show outcomes at individual, team and organizational levels of training and development activity.

Different activities will require different methods of evaluation. For example, measuring the attitude of staff towards a particular issue might effectively be captured using a questionnaire. Repeating a survey of this type after a particular event or series of changes in the workplace will help to establish the changes in attitude towards such change. This type of survey is often used in companies where a cultural shift has been sought and can be an effective tool to capture the strength of feeling towards this. It will also establish how effective managers have been in making the desired changes.

**Different methods of evaluation**

Peer appraisal, upward appraisal or appraisal by a line manager can assist in identifying individual training or development needs. Personal development planning, learning logs or updated CVs can also record and identify training and development needs and the outcomes achieved as a result of this activity and can be used to evaluate the benefits gained.

Statistical information, like that discussed above, can prove invaluable in measuring changes.

Often the methods used to evaluate the value of training and development will be determined by the activity itself. For example, a major health and safety campaign aimed at reducing accidents in the workplace could be measured by the reduction in recorded accidents. The converse of this, that is, an increase in the number of recorded accidents, could reflect the increased awareness of health and safety if this result is sustained over a short period. If this trend were to continue, it would indicate that the training did not achieve the desired effect and would point to a new training and development need. The evaluation would have been effective in measuring the changes and in highlighting a new need, even though the initial activity did not achieve what it set out to do. The evaluation process used was sufficiently robust to capture this information.

## Are we all pulling in the same direction?

While watching the opening ceremony of the Olympic Games, most people marvel at the sight of hundreds of people who by moving in a particular fashion, create a large mosaic picture of flags and symbols representing the games. Each player has a role to fulfil and through a series of simple manoeuvres creates an impact upon the group's activity. If one or two people make a mistake it is immediately obvious and the overall impact is lessened. At this level of activity each player is only conscious that they are part of a greater whole and have a limited input to the design and implementation of the plan that was developed to create the end result.

**Relate activities to the goals of the company**

In the workplace, employers have the choice of involving staff in the development of the plan for their business or in directing them towards a series of relatively simple tasks that will make the plan work. The Investors in People philosophy encourages employers to tap into the abilities and skills of staff to create and deliver actions that will ensure success. When individuals know the effect they have on the whole plan (or that part of it that directly affects them) they can appreciate the significance of their actions and often develop ways of making their contributions stronger.

The National Standard requires each company to create a written plan for the business. This plan must state the goals and targets it wishes to achieve and, crucially, it must determine what skills are required to put the plan into action. Doing this sets the scene for employers; it gives them a broad set of guidelines that will help them make decisions about the behaviours and attitudes in the workplace. This is only the start point. To ensure that all employees know what is expected of them, individuals must be able to relate their activities to the goals of the company. To do so, employers must help employees to make the connection between their individual actions and the company's goals. Setting targets and objectives that link directly to the business goals and targets will assist in this process. For example:

**Business goal:** To reduce waste by 2 per cent over the next 12 months.

**Team goal:** Each team should identify areas of waste and possible methods of reduction.

This team goal can be further developed into individual goals so that each person is responsible for the identification of waste and methods of reducing this.

In a factory setting this may be relatively straightforward; for example, the use of materials can be tracked and decisions about the use of particular types of material can result in substantial savings. A manufacturer of corrugated paper successfully reduced waste by 1 per cent simply by changing the type of paste used in the gluing process. In the office waste reduction can also be affected. Investors in People Scotland reduced the amount of paper usage through the installation of modem links from satellite offices to the head office. This system had the added advantage of increasing the speed of communications and the accessibility of information.

**The cumulative effect of 'pulling together'**

By cascading business goals and targets, as above, this will ensure that everyone understands the importance of their activities and how this affects the company as a whole. It shows them that they are important and that their efforts matter. Most importantly, it focuses individuals' actions in the direction that the company wishes to go: everyone is pulling together through a series of individual activities. Individuals recognize that they have an important role to play and that their efforts can make a difference: just like the players at the opening ceremony of the Olympic Games, only much more empowered, as they are actively contributing to business processes.

## Individuals, teams and the organization

Organizations are made up of people. The word organization is simply a convenient collective term used to describe individuals that form to make up a particular group or company. Recognizing this, the National Standard considers evaluation at three levels. Earlier in the book we have considered these levels and have seen examples of how this can work in practice. In this section we will consider why it is important to evaluate on these levels and how this can be achieved.

Using the Investors in People process, organizations can move towards a learning culture where the efforts of teams build upon the performance, initiative and achievement of individuals. Most organizations focus on individual achievement and reward this. The Investors in People process complements this but goes further. It recognizes the synergy that teams create and helps organizations to use this synergy to achieve the results they are aiming for.

**A learning culture**

Setting team objectives creates an environment in which individuals' contributions count for more than the individual effort. Teams have the additional benefit of providing an ideal environment through which people can learn from each other: a cost-effective method to develop staff.

Evaluation of team objectives means that team objectives have to be set. This does not mean that individual objectives cannot be set: the two are mutually supportive, not mutually exclusive. For example, a team objective might be to reduce wastage by 2 per cent. The team is responsible for this objective and it should complement the objectives of the individuals within the team. So, one member of the team might be responsible for identifying areas of waste while another member is looking at procedures that could be improved (to reduce waste, increase efficiency or to improve customer satisfaction levels). Broad objectives (like those above) must be made specific or SMART. In doing so the evaluation process is simplified.

**SMART objectives**

*Team objective*

**S**pecific:      Reduce waste by 2 per cent.

**M**easurable:      Waste reduced from £10,000 to £9,800 per annum.

**A**chievable:      Current waste levels are higher than believed necessary; waste reduction of 2 per cent would increase profits and reduce costs of sales. The waste levels fluctuate over each month and a 2 per cent reduction can be achieved in 'good' months. The aim is to maintain this level of reduction all year round.

**R**ealistic:      A 3 per cent reduction has been achieved in previous months. It is appropriate to aim at a 2 per cent reduction on a consistent basis; however, this will be monitored over the next quarter to ensure that the target is realistic.

**T**imebound:      The timescale for the objective is 12 months. Monthly analysis will track progress and the target of 2 per cent will be reviewed on a quarterly basis.

The above example illustrates a SMART objective and each individual objective that supports this team objective would be broken down in the same manner.

The interdependence of team and individual objectives will ensure the necessary support to achieve results. Mutually exclusive objectives create conflict and disharmony, resulting in non-achievement for many and consequently failure or reduced success of organizational objectives. So, with the team objectives set, individual objectives should be made clear. Also, the overall link between these objectives and the company's written plan should be explicit. In the example used, individual objectives could include:

*Individual objective*

**S**pecific:      Identify sources of waste in the office/shopfloor/canteen environment.

**M**easurable:      Identify between two and four sources of waste in the allocated environment within the first quarter of the financial year.

**A**chievable:      Wastage occurs in all areas at present, but as this has not been monitored closely in the past we are unsure of the level of waste. It is reasonable to assume that the target set is achievable but this will be monitored throughout the review period.

**R**ealistic:      Where waste measurements have been taken, this has been recorded at 3 to 4 per cent of material usage.

Timebound: Monthly reports will monitor progress over the first financial quarter.

Breaking organizational goals and objectives down so that these are meaningful and achievable for teams or individuals will tie the company's objectives into day-to-day activities.

## Was it worth doing?

Since any activity we embark upon aims to achieve something, we need to look back to the start of the activity and then to consider where we are now to measure 1) whether there has been any change, 2) whether the change is what we expected and 3) whether it is appropriate to the business needs. We need to consider the costs associated with such activity to ensure that value has been added to the business.

**Points to consider**

As has been shown, evaluation measures the results of tasks that have been carried out previously. The timescale attached to any particular task will help in identifying when and how this task should be measured. There is, however, a need to step back from individual tasks and look at the whole to ensure that the business is still on track to achieve its desired aims.

The National Standard requires a strategic review of the training and development to be undertaken within an organization. This approach ensures that training and development is relevant to the business needs and that the benefits gained justify the costs of this activity. It also ensures that decisions about training and development are based upon sound business decisions and not just gut feeling. The strategic human resources plan should include the cost of the plan and the method(s) of implementation. A typical human resources planning process is shown in Figure 4.4. This diagram outlines development processes and shows the links to the strategic planning process.

**A strategic review**

This model considers human resource management at a strategic level and provides the cyclical approach required by the National Standard. It is an excellent start point, with evaluation processes built in and used to strengthen and develop the business. The focus is clearly on individuals and teams.

When considering the costs of training and development these should not be restricted to the amount spent on actual 'events'. Costs should include individuals' time, salaries, materials, physical resources such as training rooms, equipment and computers, the opportunity cost of training and development and the management time used to

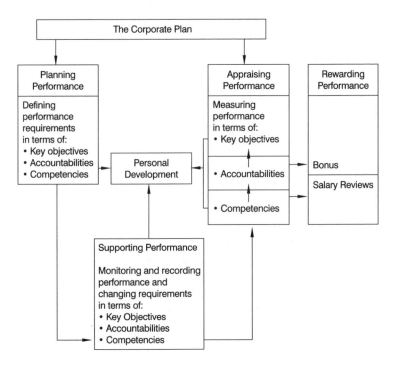

**Figure 4.4** *The performance management cycle – Scottish Widows*

plan, execute or review training activities.

Comparing these costs against turnover or payroll can give an immediate picture of the level of an organization's commitment towards the training and development of its staff. When commitment to resources is expressed as a percentage of payroll or turnover, an organization can track, on an annual basis, the level of spend in this area. There are other ways to gauge this commitment, for example the number of days spent delivering, receiving and/or participating in training and development. Again, annual comparisons assist in tracking changes in this activity.

These measures can be used to compare the value gained from training and development activity if the outcomes of this activity have been measured effectively. An example of this was shown in Crown Corrugated (Scotland) Ltd who compared the percentage of spend on training and development against the savings made in waste reduction. The company reduced waste by 1 per cent over a one-year period and gained £50,000, almost the complete budget for their training and development programme. Comparisons of this nature are useful, especially when justifying the projected budgets for training and development to board members, for example.

## Options for evaluation

How organizations evaluate a particular activity or series of activities will depend on the nature of the activity and on the method(s) of delivery. Below are some examples that have been taken from recognized organizations. These options are not exhaustive but provide an opportunity to see a variety of forms of evaluation.

---

**1. Scottish Widows**

Post-course questionnaires are used for all classroom-based activity. The analysis of these questionnaires results in courses being revised where necessary. Where individuals are working towards a professional qualification, progress is monitored through the appraisal system to ensure that the required results are being achieved.

The company has recently undertaken several major projects to evaluate the organizational culture, the prevailing management styles and the changes that will be required to ensure that the company is fit to face the future. These projects, using external consultants, have resulted in reports identifying the needs of the organization and are currently being analysed to identify the best methods of implementing the changes required.

The outcomes of training and development are evaluated at individual level through the appraisal system, at team level through the divisional plans and at the organization level through the annual report and accounts. Quality Action Teams (QATs) have been established in many departments and show impressive results where they have identified a problem or issue and have developed solutions to tackle these. QATs can apply for accreditation of their procedures through an internally developed quality assurance scheme: the Quality Accreditation Scheme.

**2. East Kilbride Business Centre**

At the individual level, certificates gained measure the results of development activity. Teams are measured against specific development activities linked to training or development, for example the speed of response to client enquiries, success of grant applications, or increased business.

---

A selling skills course undertaken by project executives resulted in greater confidence to approach clients with details of services offered, a more structured approach to selling of services, a clearer understanding of sales techniques and a clear appreciation of the difficulties surrounding sales.

At an organizational level, skills development of staff is tracked back to business goals and subsequent developments. A clear example of this is the Business Shop. The business goal was to expand services provided to businesses within the East Kilbride area as the Development Corporation will soon be closed and the restructuring of local government creates a large gap in the marketplace. Companies need to have a support mechanism in place to take on the functions previously catered for by these bodies. The development of two staff members secured the Business Shop, the first step in filling this gap.

### 3. Nabors Oil and Drilling

Nabors' approach to organizational evaluation is through continuous quality improvement. Training and development within Nabors is evaluated to ensure that it is relevant to the business objectives, for example the successful retention of the Chevron (Alba) contract. This contract was awarded in September 1993 by Chevron UK Ltd. Chevron were impressed by the Safety Management System, accreditation of BSENISO9000/BS5750, the low incident rate and the quality of the workforce.

The business plan had identified that the development of a multi-skilling training programme would enable the company to provide a more attractive and cost-effective service to the client.

A further example of evaluation is the intensive training on safety. The company Loss Time Incident rate was reduced from 3.50 in January 1993 to 1.22 in December 1993; this is the lowest incident rate ever achieved by Nabors and follows a period of wide-ranging training initiatives on safety. The incident rate rose initially, as a result of increased awareness, but over a period of several months, fell to a record low.

Individual training actions are evaluated by course assessment forms, written and practical tests and observation by managers, which is recorded formally at appraisal.

The Safety Training Observation Programme (STOP) is an example of continuous evaluation of training. STOP requires all supervisors to observe the safety practices of their staff, work procedures and equipment. Deficiencies are recorded and organizational or training actions are taken to rectify the situation.

The appraisal scheme is used to evaluate individual training actions. It is an opportunity for the supervisor to review the training and performance of the past year and comment on training gaps that still remain.

The outcomes of training and development are evaluated at organizational level through fortnightly senior management team meetings, quarterly continuous quality improvement meetings, and annual management review meetings.

In addition, the outcomes of the training programme are discussed by the training coordinator at his weekly departmental meeting. Other examples of evaluation provided by Nabors included:

- survey results that showed 59 per cent of employees were aware of company training programmes. Believing that this could be improved, the company plans to introduce a newsletter which will cover training matters;
- a skilled, flexible and committed workforce, who can meet business objectives and fulfil client expectations;
- low labour turnover of 7.8 per cent – the industry average is 13 per cent;
- a number of internal promotions, for example Roustabout to Floorman, Floorman to Lead Floorman, Lead Floorman to Derrickman, Derrickman to Assistant Driller, Assistant Driller to Driller, Driller to Assistant Rig Superintendent, and Assistant Rig Superintendent to Rig Superintendent.

Before the booking of each course, the expected benefits are detailed both for the employee and for the company on the training request form. During the annual performance appraisal interview, improvements in the competence of the personnel are recorded and training and development benefits recognized.

Department budgets are compiled by managers and this assists in their awareness of the associated costs.

Staff briefings continuously reinforce the message that the company is committed to training and development and the president/managing director frequently visits staff on offshore installations and throughout the office to promote the company mission to have a well-trained quality staff.

### 4. Simclar International Ltd

The company operates statistical process control (SPC), manufacturing resource planning II (MRP II) and total quality control (TQC) and are Part 2 BS5750, ISO9002 and EN29002 approved. Examples of evaluation at all levels were:

- *Individual.* Several individuals undertaking external qualifications and a large number of individuals who have progressed through the organization to senior levels.
- *Team.* Six Sigma sub-systems are 'owned' by managers and their team. The results are monitored internally by managers and by Motorola. Clear progression has been made in all of the nine active sub-system areas.
- *Organizational.* Simclar has developed into a major player in the sub-contracting field and now has an annual turnover of approximately £25m.

The company's training strategy clearly identifies costs associated with training and development. The cost of quality systems used by Simclar identifies each development required at an organizational level and by department. The managing change project provided further information about costs and expected benefits.

- A quality system, Six Sigma sub-system 8 Project Plan, focuses on Total Customer Satisfaction. The project was costed at £55,000 with an expected contract gain of £1m.

The examples above are intended to provide a flavour of the approaches taken by a variety of organizations to assist you in determining the best approach for your business. There are a number of ways in which training and development activity can be evaluated and the examples show how organizations have achieved this. Each company has linked training and development to business goals and is able to show the results of this activity in improved business performance. Other examples are shown throughout this book and in the examples (headed 'Illustrations') that appear in each chapter.

## Maintaining the standard

**Becoming an Investor in People**

The practices that have been outlined in this book will provide a pathway to gaining recognition as an Investor in People. Assessment against the National Standard is discussed in the next chapter. Even if formal assessment is not the preferred route, the principles and practices that a company adopts on their journey will make them stronger. Given this, it is sensible to maintain these approaches and where possible improve them.

Maintenance of the Standard begins with the planning function and the strategic review processes that by now should be well established. The written plan for the business contains the human resource strategy for the business objectives and this is reviewed along with the business goals and objectives. Established review mechanisms at team and individual levels are aligned to the business strategy and should feed into the business's decision-making processes. Evaluation of the outcomes of training and development activity will ensure that relevant training and development is delivered and these processes will create a culture that is healthy and open. Where these practices are in place, individuals are clear about their input, how this contributes to the business and to them personally.

**A healthy and open business culture**

In this environment the National Standard is almost self-maintaining. If an organization controls the strategy for the business and puts in place supporting mechanisms to ensure that strategic drift is kept to a minimum then the National Standard will provide the framework through which to maintain this approach.

Figure 4.5 shows what maintenance of the National Standard is about.

This process is cyclical, as no part of the National Standard works in isolation.

## Still committed?

The National Standard is an effective tool that will create a number of changes within any organization that uses it. The change process will provide the impetus for business improvement and is designed to involve all staff no matter what their job is. All staff have a contribution to make to the business that employs them. The National Standard facilitates business development through people. It is the recognition of this unique resource that gives organizations their strength and that sets them apart from other organizations. Each individual is unique and has a set of skills and talents that, if used effectively, will enhance the ability of the employing organization to achieve their goals. Given that this resource is available only to the employing organization, it is common sense to use this strength to build a successful business. Many employers recognize this but struggle to find a method of tapping into this resource. The National Standard provides a tried and tested framework to do just this. Those organizations that have achieved recognition as an Investor in People are finding that their businesses

**Building on individual's strengths**

Setting business goals and targets

Reviewing business goals and targets

Establishing development activities linked to those goals and targets

Implementing development actions

Evaluating the outcomes of the development activities against planned goals and targets

Re-establishing business goals and targets: write down business objectives for an agreed period, perhaps one year

**Figure 4.5** *Maintaining the standard*

are stronger and more flexible. With nothing to lose and a lot to gain, commitment to adopt the principles of the National Standard makes business sense.

**There is no real substitute for human capital**

This is not a new concept: the resource-based theory of the firm argues that sustained competitive advantage is secured from the organization's internal resources. The criterion that these resources require to meet, before such advantage is gained, fit the human capital of an organization well. Human capital is, on the whole, unique (to the firm), difficult to imitate, not easy to substitute and is able to add value to the product or service offered. Investors in People might just be the key to how human capital can provide the holy grail of sustained competitive advantage.

The exercises presented so far in this book are designed to assist you in finding out how well your company's practices meet the requirements of the Standard and what actions you need to take to meet all of these. In the next chapter the process of assessment is outlined to assist you in taking the next step towards external recognition.

## ILLUSTRATION

### Oki

#### INTRODUCTION TO THE COMPANY

In the years since Investors in People recognition, Oki has been the recipient of the Best Electronics Factory in Britain Award (1992) and the Scottish Quality Award (1994). The DTI has included Oki in its portfolio of 'Best Practice' companies: 'Inside UK Enterprise'. As a result, the company has hosted a number of visits for other organizations, illustrating their methods and processes.

The company's philosophy of continuous improvement has seen renewed progress against a range of business measures, success in which has been frequently underpinned by attention to the development and training of the workforce. Over the past three years there have been year-on-year increases in the identification, action and participation in business-related training and development activities. A culture of learning has become embedded at Oki, and recognition of its effects has led to further investment in training.

The company's vision, created in 1990/91, reflects their aim:

*Through continuous development of our people and systems, in partnership with our customers and suppliers, to become a world-class manufacturer of high quality products.*

This vision has become a reality, as the company successfully competes against other manufacturers and internally with other Oki sites in Thailand and Japan to win orders for Cumbernauld.

#### EVALUATION: THE EVIDENCE

**4.1 The organization evaluates the impact of training and development actions on knowledge, skills and attitude.**

Course review forms are a first measure of whether development actions have met the identified needs. Production minutes regularly monitor whether training issues may be underlying achievement of daily goals. The Flat Bed Assembly (FBA) training plan and subsequent analysis of machine productivity is a clear example of evaluation of the effect of training technicians in machine maintenance on the effectiveness of their new-found skills. The appraisal process is an ongoing cycle of identification, action and review of whether development actions have met their goals. An example was also provided of an extensive review meeting on the ongoing Leadership Development Programme. A combination of the systems outlined in this indicator and those shown under 4.2 and 4.3 ensure that skills, knowledge and attitudinal changes are measured.

### 4.2 The organization evaluates the impact of training and development actions on performance.

The appraisal system, monthly and weekly review meetings, and annual objectives setting and review cycles ensure that evaluation covers individual, team and organizational levels. Quality can be impacted at all levels and training interventions are addressed at individual, team, or departmental level. For example, purchasing training was evaluated by individual contribution through the appraisal and by performance against particular commodity targets. This was monitored by reference to the performance of all buyers and by the performance of the department as a whole in achieving Purchase Price Variance (PPV) targets. Training on negotiation, purchasing and supply techniques, and developmental moves from one area of responsibility to another are seen to be contributory to these performance measures.

Specific examples of the outcomes of training and development activities are provided below:

**Individual objective**
To learn how to use computer systems more effectively.

**Business need**
To train a junior member of staff to undertake new computer-related duties to further enhance skills levels and to provide an opportunity for further development.

**Training intervention**
A comprehensive programme of network and applications training established.

**Outcome**
Formal qualification now being pursued, line manager's time freed up for other duties, job enhancement for individual concerned.

**Team objective**
To train line managers in use of new appraisal system.

**Business need**
Improve the approach to appraisals, focusing on future individual and business needs.

**Training intervention**

In-house workshops on the new appraisal procedures for all line managers, highlighting the changes to the system and reinforcing the manager's role in identifying training needs linked to business objectives. To ensure managers were able to assist staff in skills identification and training needs and highlight the benefits of further education.

**Outcome**

Increased managers' awareness of the benefits of the new appraisal system, increase in the number of staff undertaking further education training.

**Organization objective**

Identify and implement a recording mechanism for tracking personnel records.

**Business need**

Improve the quality of information and speed of access to this information relating to individual personnel records.

**Training intervention**

A Microsoft Word-compatible system for personnel administration identified and training in its use implemented.

**Outcome**

Access time for records reduced from hours to minutes. Improved quality of information and variety and style of information improved.

**4.3    The organization evaluates the contribution of training and development to the achievement of its goals and targets.**

The nature of Oki's operation is such that there is a high degree of measurement of all aspects of business operations. Quality, output, efficiency, delivery and other process-related measures are reviewed in real time or hourly in some cases, and in production meetings at the end of each day. These can generate points that feed into requirements for training interventions. There are weekly operations meetings with all functional managers and a monthly review. These meetings review progress towards business goals and targets. This is the forum for discussion of the contribution of development of people to business goals. Evidence was provided for presentations made at recent meetings that focused on training strategy, training related to product introductions, and training interventions that have resulted in quality improvements. The appraisal process also requires review of the contribution of training to business goals. The Production Awareness Training (PAT) exercise and its subsequent evaluation questionnaire are examples of the way in which the company monitors and evaluates the contribution of training activity.

**4.4 Top management understands the broad costs and benefits of training and developing employees.**

Examples of managerial input into budget planning for training shows an acute awareness of training costs, as does preparation of detailed costings for all training. The extent of investment in further education reflects a belief held at the most senior level in the organization that training is a strategic issue requiring full commitment. The recent agreement by the general manager to increase the training budget in response to demand for further education, and regular discussions regarding the contribution of training to retention of staff and improved business measures, are further evidence of the understanding of the benefits of developing people.

**4.5 Top management's continuing commitment to training and developing employees is demonstrated to all employees.**

Continuing commitment to developing people is assured through the various activities that Oki are involved with. These activities include: ongoing training activity, participation of management in the appraisal processes, discussions at Members Council and public activity such as promotion of training and development and the Investors in People standard. Articles in the company newsletter, *Okitalk*, and in the PCB area newsletter are further evidence of an awareness that the company has a continuing commitment to develop people. Oki also has an agreement with a local college to operate certificated courses on site for staff who would not be able to attend the college location. This commitment to the provision of access to training and development has been used to good effect by a large number of staff.

**4.6 Action takes place to implement improvements to training and development identified as a result of evaluation.**

The main review mechanism is the company appraisal system, which requires a formal annual review of training and development needs; however, such is the level of activity and interest that needs are often identified on a less formal basis and discussed and researched as they arise. Managers frequently consult the training officer and Personnel staff seeking sources of appropriate training. The Production Awareness Training (PAT) carried out in 1994 is an example of a major exercise in identifying a problem, constructing a programme of training, and delivering and subsequently evaluating its results. This whole process was conducted by production supervisory staff with advice from Personnel.

Another example was the unsatisfactory performance of a key piece of printed circuit board (PCB) equipment. A production team-leader identified the need for maintenance training for technicians, and following sourcing and delivery of this training, was able to demonstrate significant improvement in machine productivity.

Anticipated increases in volume have recently resulted in one process (PCB Operation Panels) being sub-contracted to another Investors in People company: Simclar Limited. Oki's strategy for this involved training Simclar employees to appropriate standards to ensure similar quality levels were achieved.

During 1994, the need to implement a manufacturing planning and control system (MAPICs) on IBM AS400 hardware was identified and a comprehensive training plan devised to support this implementation. Training needs versus business objectives are constantly under review at Oki through the Key Members Group, the Senior Management Team (SMT) and the Personnel Department. Monthly meetings of the SMT are used to review the training and development strategy against business objectives.

Throughout the reassessment of Oki (UK) Limited interviewees referred to the company culture of continuous improvement, relating this to their own skills' enhancement in the first instance. The company has created an environment in which staff are able to articulate their fears and desires and in which they are able to take up opportunity for advancement and increased opportunity.

Through the Investors in People process the company has built upon established practices and has enhanced these over the period of recognition. This determination to improve continually is further reflected in the company's desire to advance their practices to higher levels.

### Summary

The key aspects that you must address from the principle of **evaluation** are:

- identifying the processes that will be used, at the strategic level, to evaluate the human resources plan, its relevance to the business, its flexibility and the contribution that implementation of this plan will make to the business success;
- identifying the processes that will measure the outcomes of specific, individual training and development actions;
- recording the outcomes of the strategic, team and individual evaluation;
- ensuring that (senior) managers understand all costs and benefits associated with human resource development activity that takes place in the company;
- using the evaluation process to improve your business continually.

### Exercise 4.1 – Part 1

|  | Yes/ No. | Action required | What action |
|---|---|---|---|
| 1. Does your organization have a process to record and evaluate individual achievements? | | | |
| 2. Does this procedure cover all aspects of an employee's development? | | | |
| 3. Does your organization have a procedure to evaluate the effectiveness of the company training policy? | | | |
| 4. Does this evaluation cover all aspects of training and development? | | | |
| 5. Do your evaluation procedures consider achievement at individual, team and organizational levels? | | | |
| 6. Do staff understand the links between training and development received and their own job role? | | | |
| 7. Are managers aware of the costs associated with training and development? | | | |

|  | Yes/ No | Action required | What action |
|---|---|---|---|
| 8. Are managers aware of the cost of not providing proper training and development for staff? | | | |

**Exercise 4.1 – Part 2**

|  | Yes/ No | Action required | What action |
|---|---|---|---|
| 1. Does your organization have a process to record and evaluate individual achievements? | No | ✓ | Consider your HR strategy and determine the most appropri- ate evalua- tion methods. |
| 2. Does this procedure cover all aspects of an employee's development? | No | ✓ | Consider evaluation on three levels: individual, team and organiza- tional. |
| 3. Does your organization have a procedure to evaluate the effectiveness of the company processes training policy? | No | ✓ | Look back at your review and consider how these support evaluation at a strat- egic level. |
| 4. Does this evaluation cover all aspects of training and development? | No | ✓ | Consider how clear your HR strategy is. |

# ◀ CHAPTER 5 ▶

# THE ASSESSMENT
# PROCESS

*Je ne cherche pas, je trouve (I do not seek, I find).*

Pablo Picasso, Spanish artist

**Assessment and training is a cyclical process**

## Outline of the process

In this chapter, I want to remind you that the National Standard is not about best practice, it is about good practice. The National Standard is a business development tool that, when used effectively, will deliver economic benefits to you and your staff. The National Standard reflects good business practice: that is, if you employ individuals to do a job, they need to know what is expected of them and they should be trained, if required, to do that job. Their performance in the job should be monitored and where any deficiencies in job performance are noted, action to fill these gaps taken. Ongoing monitoring should take place within the organization to ensure that skills are effective and that all activity within the business is focused on achieving the objectives that the organization has set itself. This process is cyclical. So training and development is focused on those who need it and is measured against the achievement of business objectives.

If an organization wishes to gain external recognition for these activities, they can opt to be assessed, in Scotland, by Investors in People Scotland or by the network of Assessors in England, Ireland and Wales. In each case, your first point of contact should be with either your Local Enterprise Company (LEC) in Scotland or your Training Enterprise Council (TEC) in England, Ireland or Wales. Each of these bodies will provide information on how to apply for assessment.

The following information is intended as a guide on how to pull together the information you will require for assessment. This chapter and the appendices provide further information on the assessment process. This information is based on the practices of Investors in People Scotland, but is applicable across the whole of the United Kingdom.

Investors in People Scotland has produced an Assessment Framework that provides clear information on the whole assessment process. This chapter cannot provide you with the same level of detail, but a few tips that may help you through the process are outlined below. Although it is not meant to be an exhaustive list it will help you to understand how a typical assessment would be carried out. All practices are based on those operated by Investors in People Scotland, but mirror those used throughout the country:

**The assessment process**

- You agree with your LEC/TEC that you meet all of the indicators of the National Standard and that you would like to be assessed and recognized as an Investor in People.
- Your LEC/TEC contact books your company for assessment.
- An Investors in People Assessor is allocated to your company and contacts your LEC/TEC to confirm details.
- Your Assessor now contacts you directly to arrange the assessment, confirm suitable dates and check any final details.
- A pre-assessment meeting or telephone call will check:
  - dates of the assessment;
  - number of employees;
  - number of sites that your company has;
  - whether you have completed your storyboard and collected any relevant evidence;
  - discuss with you the likely costs; and
  - explain in detail the process of assessment.
- Details of costs and timescales will be confirmed in writing to you after this discussion.

- The first day of the assessment will begin with the Assessor analysing all the documentary evidence you have provided, including your storyboard. An assessment plan will be drawn up and will detail, by name, those individuals who have been selected for interview and the length of time that each interview will take. Your Assessor will check the availability of staff with you and try to accommodate your business requirements as best as possible. Interviews can be undertaken individually or in groups. Your Assessor will decide on the best methods and discuss the implications of these with you.

- All interviews are confidential and an analysis of this information together with that collected from the documentation provided by your company will be undertaken off site.

- The Assessor will compile a report presenting your case and making a recommendation. If this recommendation is positive, your report will be presented to a Recognition Panel within four weeks (in Scotland – timescales vary in other parts of the country) of the analysis. It is the Recognition Panel that makes the decision to recognize a company or not. The Assessor makes a recommendation only and provides verbal evidence to support his or her decision at the Panel meeting.

- If the Panel accepts the Assessor's recommendation your LEC/TEC representative will be informed and instructed to pass on the news to you.

- A feedback meeting or discussion with your Assessor will guide you through the Recognition Panel Report and inform you of the Panel's decision. This meeting is also used to provide you with any other relevant information.

- Recognition is granted on the basis that a programme of ongoing review and assessment will take place. Your Assessor will book your reassessment and provide you with the options available to you when he or she writes to confirm the Recognition Panel feedback.

Where the Assessor is not making a positive recommendation, the report will detail what additional work is required by the company to gain the National Standard and at the feedback meeting your Assessor will discuss with you the likely timescales attached to any activity you undertake.

The above is a brief outline of the process and is not intended to substitute for any advice that may be available from your LEC/TEC to guide you through the process.

## Audit trail/questions

Below is a list of typical questions and issues that the Assessor is likely to probe during an assessment. The list is not exhaustive and is a representation of the general areas that an assessment would cover. Beside each question is an indicator number. This represents the area of the National Standard that is directly related to the question being asked. Beside this, in the second column, a list of related indicators are presented.

You will see that there is a great deal of cross-over between many of the questions and corresponding indicators. This is because no one system or process stands in isolation and so different parts of the Standard will be affected by these. The audit trail will help you to understand how different parts of the Standard link together.

It will help to keep a copy of the Standard with you when reading though this section.

| Questions/Issues | Immediate indicator | Associated indicator |
|---|---|---|
| What goals are set out in the written business plan? | (Indicator 2.1) | all indicators |
| What targets were established for these goals | (indicator 2.1) | all indicators |
| What broad development needs arose from the goals and targets? | (indicator 2.2) | 2.4, 4.3 and 4.4 |
| How were these development needs identified? | (indicator 2.2) | 2.3, 3.3 and 3.5 |
| How will these development needs be met? | (indicator 2.2) | 2.4, 2.3, 3.3 and 3.6 |
| What resources will be used to meet these development needs? | (indicator 2.4) | 4.4 |
| How were the broad development needs translated into individual needs? | (indicators 2.3 and 3.6) | 2.2 |
| What processes are used to monitor the relevance of the broad development needs that have been identified from the business goals? | (indicators 2.2, 2.3 and 4.3) | 4.1 |
| How often does this happen? | (indicators 2.2, 2.3) | 2.1, 2.4 |
| Who is involved in this process? | (indicators 2.2, 2.3) | 1.1, 2.4 and 3.2 |

| Questions/Issues | Immediate indicator | Associated indicator |
|---|---|---|
| What development actions have taken place as a result of the planning process? | (indicators 3.2, 3.6) | 4.1, 4.3 and 4.6 |
| What impact did this activity have on the business? | (indicator 4.1) | 2.6 and 2.1 |
| What effect did the actions taken have on the business goals and targets that were established in the business plan? | (indicator 4.3) | 2.1, 2.2, 3.2 3.6 and 4.6 |
| What effect did the development activity have on individuals? | (indicator 4.2) | 2.3 3.2 and 3.4 |
| What effect did the development activity have on teams? | (indicator 4.2) | 2.1, 2.2 and 2.6 |
| What effect did the development activity have on the whole company? | (indicator 4.2) | 2.1, 2.2, 2.6, 4.5 and 4.6 |
| How much (£) was spent on this activity? | (indicator 4.4) | 2.4 |
| Was the activity worthwhile? | (indicator 4.4) | 2.1, 2.2, and 2.4 |
| How did the company justify the spend on the development activity? | (indicator 4.4) | 2.2, 2.3, 2.4, 4.1, 4.2 and 4.3 |

## Autonomy

### List of typical questions/issues to probe

**A general guide to assessment**

The following section is aimed towards organizations that are part of a group of companies and is only a general guide on those issues that may be probed during the assessment to determine whether the organization has the authority to be assessed as a separate unit. Your LEC/TEC representative is able to help you to determine any specific authority issues you may have.

The Assessor may wish to discuss the following to determine whether your organization is autonomous:

- Does the organization have a business plan that relates specifically to the site to be assessed?
- How is the business plan devised, who is involved and how is the plan 'signed off' with the parent group?
- What is the pricing policy of the organization, for the group and the site? How is this determined?

- How are the profits of the organization used? Can the site retain these profits to reinvest or are they given back to the parent?

**Note:** Either situation can occur; however, it is essential that this is clearly explained and that the level of control exercised from the parent company upon the site being assessed is explicit.

- How does the site gain new business? If the main supplier of business is the parent company it is essential that the process of how this business is gained is made clear. For example, many organizations bid internally for contracts from their parent group. If bids are made for business, this should be explained and to support the issue of authority, it may be useful to include information on past contracts that the site has not tendered for or indeed where they have tendered but have been unsuccessful.
- What level of control does the site have in terms of decision making, particularly around the level and type of business, the methods used to support staff and procedural issues?
- How is the budget for the site determined, who is involved, how is this allocated?
- Is there evidence of delegated authority for the site to pursue Investors in People?

The questions above focus on the decision-making processes that are present in any company. Through discussion with the management team, the Assessor will determine whether the site being assessed is autonomous.

## Other autonomy issues
The following information is intended to assist you in identifying other issues that may help to determine authority. For example, does the site:

- have a separate image/identity?
- have a separate legal identity?
- management have the authority to hire and fire staff?
- management have authority to set the staffing complement?
- management have the authority to determine the terms and conditions of staff?

Using some or all of the questions presented in the next exercise, you can help provide the Assessor with information on the autonomy of your business. There are no pre-set answers to any of these questions. The correct answer is what happens in your business.

**Exercise 5.1 – Part 1**

| Questions | Answers |
|---|---|
| 1. Does the site have a written business plan that is specific to that site? | |
| 2. Does the plan meet the Investors in People criteria, that is, does it meet 2.1, 2.2, 2.3, 2.4, and 4.3? | |
| 3. Does the site have authority to change practices (not necessarily policies) for the human resource management of the site? | |
| 4. Does the site have authority over its budget, in relation to the human resources? | |
| 5. How is the business plan drawn up? | |
| 6. Who is involved in this process? | |
| 7. How is it integrated with the group/parent company strategy? | |
| 8. What happens where disagreements occur? | |
| 9. How are these disagreements resolved? | |
| 10. How is the business plan 'signed off' by the group/parent company? | |
| 11. Is the group/parent company committed to Investors in People? | |
| 12. Is there any evidence of this commitment? | |
| 13. What level of input to the day-to-day business does the group/parent company have? | |

## Presenting the portfolio

Portfolio: portable case for loose papers/drawings: a collection of such papers

*Chambers English Dictionary*

**What is a portfolio?**

The term 'portfolio of evidence' is commonly used by LEC/TEC staff, consultants and Assessors to describe the information that a company uses to present their case for assessment against the National Standard. Typically, a portfolio of evidence will contain a storyboard, similar to the ones shown at the end of this chapter, a current business plan or strategy document and a variety of items of documentary evidence to support their submission for assessment.

The portfolio of evidence is the Assessor's guide to your company, its policies and practices and the evidence that supports your application for recognition as an Investor in People. Normally, the Assessor will have no previous knowledge of your company, so it is essential that the information you present is clear and complete.

The Assessor will use the portfolio to make an initial judgement about whether the policies and practices that your company applies meet the requirements of the National Standard. This is the start of the assessment process, so all of the information that you wish to present should be contained in this document.

Below are some guidelines and tips on how to present this evidence. This is meant to guide you through the process of presenting your evidence and is based upon the practices of a number of recognized companies. Remember, the portfolio is like an induction pack for a member of the senior management team: it should contain sufficient information to tell the complete story of how your company meets the requirements of the National Standard. Typically a portfolio will contain: an overview of the company (the storyboard), the business plan which should contain information about resources and one or two key documents which relate to the main business processes, for example performance review documentation.

**A portfolio is the Assessor's 'induction pack' to your company**

## Alternatives to the portfolio

There has never been a requirement to produce a portfolio; however, when they first apply for formal assessment many organizations do so to assist the Assessor. At either the first assessment or later, during subsequent reviews, there are alternative ways to ensure the assessment process runs smoothly. For an assessment against the National Standard, all organizations are required to have a written plan that reflects the organization's goals and objectives. This plan (or separate but related plans) must include details of training and development requirements for all employees and how these needs will be resourced.

Naturally then, for an assessment these are the only documents that an organization needs to facilitate the assessment process. If this approach appeals to you, you need to be prepared to assist the Assessor at the planning stage with the following information:

- the number of employees and the types of jobs they do;
- the number of sites your organization has;
- when you want the assessment to begin;
- the type of report you would prefer (see below for details);
- when you want the next assessment to take place.

The process of assessment has always been designed to be as flexible as possible and geared towards creating minimum disruption to the day-to-day operations of the organization being assessed. By providing employers with greater involvement in the design of the assessment, the report style, feedback and subsequent assessments, the aim is to improve the overall process.

## The assessment report

Reports produced as a result of a formal assessment against the National Standard need to provide clear information about those aspects of the organization's practices that meet the Standard's requirements and those that don't. This is still the case regardless of the type of assessment your organization chooses. The style of the report can, however, be customized to reflect individual organizational needs. For example, a report can be written using key business processes, such as communication and business planning to show where an organization stands against the National Standard. Alternatively, a report may show the audit trails the Assessor used during the site visit to reflect this information. The traditional style using each indicator can also be selected and this option may be most suitable for a first-time assessment.

## The timing of assessments

Initially, organizations that were assessed against the National Standard and found to meet all of its requirements were recognized for a period of three years. Feedback from employers suggested that more frequent assessments that focused on improvement areas would assist in creating the sought-after cycle of continuous improvement. As a result, organizations can now choose when they wish to be assessed at any time during the first three years, but are still required to have at least one formal assessment by the end of the three-year period. In effect, the choice is to be assessed at least once every three years or more frequently during this period. Whichever choice is made, the focus of the assessment remains a judgement of how well the organization's practices meet the National Standard's requirements and what actions can be taken to improve those practices.

## The storyboard

If the choice made by your organization is to create a portfolio for your assessment you may wish to produce a storyboard. The storyboard is that part of your portfolio that explains how your company meets the requirements of the National Standard. The illustrations used throughout this book and the examples given at the end of this chapter are extracts from companies who have achieved recognition against the Standard. These illustrations show storyboards which are written using the National Standard's indicators as the prompt under which processes are described. If you prefer you can describe processes and leave it to the Assessor or LEC/TEC Advisor to make the comparisons with the National Standard for you. In Chapter 6, the illustration used is based on the European Foundation for Quality Management Excellence Model and linkages to IIP are highlighted throughout the illustration. Whichever method you select to present your case, you should begin by introducing your company to the Assessor. You should include:

- information about the products and services that you offer;
- a brief history of the company;
- details of your main customers;
- recent development activities and current employment levels.

It may be possible to use marketing materials that you have produced to present this part of the storyboard as these often contain the type of information an Assessor will need to begin the process of analysing your company against the National Standard.

Next you need to select your approach to the main part of the storyboard. If you choose to use the indicators of the National Standard to lead, you will need to look at each indicator in turn, writing down, in two or three sentences, how your company meets each indicator and then list any documentary evidence you have to support your statements.

**Use documentary evidence as a support**

For example:

## Indicator 2.1

A written but flexible plan sets out the organization's goals and targets.

## Supporting statement

ABC Co. Ltd produces a three-year strategic plan for the business that sets out our long-term goals. An annual operating plan is produced in September of each year to ensure that appropriate targets are established to meet these goals. The senior management team, consisting of the managing director and five other directors, review both of these documents, annually and bi-monthly respectively.

### Supporting evidence

(a) Three-year strategic plan 1993–1996 REF 1
(b) Annual operating plan 1994 REF 2
(c) Minutes from the senior management team bi-monthly annual operating plan meeting REF 3
(d) Minutes from the senior management team annual strategic plan meeting. REF 4

Repeat this for all 23 indicators. When you have completed this exercise, you will have created a storyboard and a very effective summary of the policies and practices your company uses to meet the National Standard, or will have identified gaps that still exist.

The next part of the process is to collect all the evidence that you listed in your storyboard and clearly mark it with a reference number or letter to tie it into the appropriate indicator (see above). This process is useful as it ensures that you have checked each indicator and satisfied yourself that your company does meet the requirements of the Standard. By producing a matrix of written evidence you are cross-checking that you are presenting the best evidence that exists. Examples of such a matrix of written evidence are shown in the illustration at the end of this chapter (pages 102–22).

**A matrix of written evidence**

By using a matrix of written evidence a picture of the supporting information for each indicator can be created. The Assessor will use this to assist in the assessment process.

## The appendices

**Keep appendices to a minimum**

Appendices should be kept to a minimum, wherever possible. The Assessor will have to read the documentation you produce and as there is a cost associated with the assessment process it is in your interest to make sure that only relevant information is presented. Appendices normally include those items listed in the Matrix of Written Evidence, which is a summary of those items listed throughout your storyboard. You will see from the illustrated matrix that the documents presented are all produced as part of normal business activities: not created for the purposes of assessment. The use of such naturally occurring business documentation means that you should be able to pull together current information for the assessment without major development work.

**Additional considerations**

There are a number of additional items of evidence that the Assessor will need to conduct the assessment. These should be included in the portfolio, either as appendices or contained within the body of the storyboard. These are:

- a list of all employees (*where possible, it is of value to the Assessor if you provide a list of employees that shows the length of service, gender and the job title of each individual*);
- location of the company's site(s);
- an organizational chart or a description of the structure of the company.

Where your organization is part of a group or a larger company it is essential that the Assessor is aware of this. A simple method of providing this information is often to describe the links with the parent company and to explain the decision-making processes used to develop and implement the business plan. This information can be included in the storyboard or as an appendix in the portfolio.

**Describe links with the parent company, if any**

If you choose to describe the business processes used in your company as the best method to create your storyboard you will need to check that you have provided information to cover all parts of the National Standard. In Chapter 6 the illustration shows how you can do this.

## The assessment visit

The length of an assessment visit will depend upon the size and structure of the business. Prior to conducting the assessment the Assessor will provide an estimate of the time it will take to carry out the process. This information is based upon the number of employees, the number of sites included in the assessment, the structure of the company and the type of business operation. The estimate may change, but the Assessor will inform you of any changes as the process begins. Where additional evidence is required, either in documentary form or through additional interviews, the Assessor will explain why this is necessary and what is required. The Assessor will ask to tour the site(s) being assessed as this tour can provide additional evidence to support the application for recognition as an Investor in People.

## What does the assessor do?

The assessment process is split into a number of distinct parts. Each of these parts is outlined below.

### Planning the assessment

The request for assessment is received and the Assessor will contact the company to check the details provided and arrange suitable dates for the assessment visit. During this initial conversation the Assessor will

**Planning visits**

confirm that the company is aware of the processes to be used and that supporting evidence is available. The Assessor may visit your company prior to the assessment to finalize arrangements and discuss in detail all aspects of the process. This normally happens in larger organizations or where a complicated assessment is envisaged. This is often referred to as a pre-assessment visit/discussion.

*Confirming the cost*

**Scoping**

After an initial discussion or visit, the Assessor will write to confirm the costs of the assessment. This cost is based upon the scoping exercise that has been conducted during the pre-assessment visit/discussion. Scoping is the term used to confirm the number of employees, the number and location of the sites and the process of identifying those people who will be selected for interview. If during the assessment it is clear that additional time is required the Assessor will agree this with you.

*Conducting the assessment*

**Overview**

The Assessor will arrive on the day and time agreed with you to begin the analysis of the portfolio of evidence. This process takes, on average, one day. The analysis of this information provides the Assessor with an overview of the policies and procedures used in the company and highlights areas that will be probed during the next stage of the assessment. The Assessor will use the list of employees and the organizational chart to select individuals for interview. Often the selection of interviewees will begin at the pre-assessment stage.

*The interviews*

**Confidentiality**

The Assessor will select individuals for interview and provide a schedule for the interview process. The Assessor will discuss this schedule with you to ensure that it is achievable and will cause minimum disruption to business operations. Interviewees will be informed that all interviews are confidential, that written notes will be taken by the Assessor and that where group interviews are used, individuals need not speak about issues that they would be uncomfortable discussing in front of colleagues. Where this occurs, the Assessor may follow up with a one-to-one discussion.

Each interview is analysed against the indicators of the National Standard and the Assessor makes a judgement about whether or not the company meets the required standard. The schedule of interviews may be extended to include additional staff where insufficient or conflicting evidence has been gathered. The interview process must generate enough evidence to support the Assessor's recommendation.

Interviews are designed to:

- confirm the application of policies and procedures described in the portfolio of evidence;
- gather supporting information about the consistency of application of these policies and procedures;
- clarify the Assessor's understanding of policies and procedures;
- add to the quality of the information gathered from the analysis of the portfolio of evidence.

*Analysing the evidence*

After analysing the portfolio of evidence and having conducted the interviews the Assessor needs to synthesize these analyses. This normally takes place off-site. It is not normally possible for the Assessor to provide a decision at the end of the interview stage of the process. This is partly because the interview analysis takes time, but most importantly, the Assessor needs to reflect on the findings of the portfolio and interview evidence and the analysis of these two sets of information.

## What happens next?

After the analysis of the portfolio and the interview evidence has been completed the Assessor will make a judgement about whether the company meets the requirements of the National Standard. The Assessor will produce a report to support this decision and will make a recommendation to the Recognition Panel about the company.

**The Assessor's report**

## The Recognition Panel

Currently, in Scotland, Recognition Panels meet twice per month at a number of different locations. In England, Wales and Ireland, frequency will vary. The Recognition Panel is the decision-making body and has responsibility for ensuring consistency in the assessment process. Panel members are drawn from recognized companies and Panels comprise a senior person from each company.

The Panel meeting normally consists of between three and four members, although recent developments in the Panel process have seen the number of members per Panel reduced to two. Prior to the meeting (normally five working days) the Assessor's Report will be issued to each participating member who will read the report and list any issues that they may wish to discuss with the Assessor. At the Panel meeting, the Assessor will present his or her case for the company and invite questions from the Panel. Each member will ask the Assessor questions to satisfy him/herself that the Assessor has made the correct recommendation and to ensure that the assessment was conducted in the appropriate manner. After this discussion, the Panel will decide whether the company should be recognized. There are a number of decision options open to the Panel at this time.

*Recognition*

The Panel accepts the Assessor's recommendation and the company is recognized as an Investor in People.

*Not recommended*

The Panel does not accept the Assessor's recommendation and will not recognize the company. Where this situation occurs, the Panel must make explicit what the company must do to reach the requirements of the National Standard. Where this option is exercised a timescale for action will normally be agreed between the Assessor and the company concerned. Where this has happened in the past, it normally relates to additional evidence being required to satisfy the Panel on a particular point, for example the length of time a particular process has been in operation.

## Options available to organizations 'not yet ready'

**Obtaining assistance**

Where the Assessor has judged that a company does not meet the requirements of the National Standard, he or she will provide the company with clear information on what areas of the Standard are not yet met and will agree a timescale for the return visit to finalize the assessment. Assessors do not provide assistance in implementing or devising plans to meet the Standard. This is the responsibility of the company and assistance is available through the LEC and TEC network. Many companies prefer to use their own expertise or to combine this with the assistance available through the LEC/TEC network. External consultants are often used either to provide assistance with one-off activities or to assist in the changes associated with the Investor in People process. Each company should choose the option that they feel is most appropriate to their needs. LEC and TEC staff are trained in the requirements of the National Standard and can provide valuable assistance.

Upon completion of the development activities that have been out-lined by the Assessor's report, the company will be reassessed against the National Standard. Where only minor development actions have been required and the timescale is short, for example up to six months, only those outstanding parts of the Standard will be reassessed. Where development actions take longer than this timescale the company will be reassessed against the whole of the National Standard. Each company will be advised individually by the Assessor of the implications of not meeting all of the requirements in the first instance.

**Full reassessment is not always necessary**

## Beyond recognition

Feedback after the Panel is provided in the form of the Assessor's report and through discussion. The Assessor will pass on any com-ments that the Panel have asked should be disclosed and provide a summary of their findings. The Assessor does not normally provide 'consultancy' advice unless this advice has direct relevance to the maintenance of the Standard. This feedback normally relates to issues that, if not carefully monitored, could fall below the requirements of the Standard. If such a lapse were to occur, recognition would be jeopardized.

**The period of recognition is normally three years**

Reassessment is explained below; however, it should be noted that there has been a change to the period of recognition. Previously com-panies would have been recognized for a period of three years. However, a move to recognizing an organization for life with frequent review visits has recently been introduced. The next section explains the changes to the period of recognition and builds on the informa-tion presented earlier in this chapter. Regardless of the change in approach to the period of recognition, Investor in People companies are, and always have been, expected to maintain the practices used to achieve recognition and where possible to use their evaluation pro-cesses to identify areas of improvement. This process of continuous improvement is at the heart of the National Standard and has always been a fundamental principle upon which Investor in People is founded.

## The reassessment process

The reassessment of a company against the National Standard can mirror the initial assessment process or can now take the form of a review and development visit. These options are explained below.

## Options for reassessment

*The three-year review*

Analysis of the portfolio of evidence and interviews results in an assessment report that makes a recommendation to the Recognition Panel. It is useful to highlight changes in practices and procedures to the Assessor in any new portfolio or at the initial planning meeting and to indicate the impact that these changes have had on the company during the recognition period. Where feedback from the original assessment highlighted development areas, it is worth explaining to the Assessor what action has been taken to address these issues. If no action has been taken, explain why not; for example, there may have been changes in the market that made revision of a practice unnecessary.

The local LEC/TEC Advisor will assist you in preparing for reassessment by producing with you a list of changes to your organization. The three year reassessment process comprises: preparation, on-site review by the Assessor, and feedback to you after the Recognition Panel has had time to read the Assessor's report and probe with the Assessor any issues they may have.

*Variable review timeframes*

**Highlight any changes and improvements**

Variable review timeframes have been introduced to provide flexibility within the assessment process. Many recognized companies find that the timing of the three-year cycle of assessment falls at a particularly busy period and can create difficulties for assessment. Common reasons for wishing to move the assessment dates are to provide better access to employees or to minimize disruption to business. Now with the option of a flexible approach to the review process the option of changing dates is available.

This approach also comprises of preparation, on-site activity and feedback. The key differences, apart from the timescales involved, are:

- no portfolio is required – just a current business plan, organizational chart/list of employees and a note of any significant changes since the last Assessor visit;
- shorter on-site visit, focusing on the changes since the previous assessment;
- interviews start with the most senior person in the company;
- audit trails followed by the Assessor while on site may change as a result of interviewees' responses to questioning;

- feedback is immediate – there is no waiting for a Recognition Panel to verify the Assessor's judgement;
- report is verified by the assessment unit and a copy sent to the company.

So, what are the differences between the two? The chart shown in Table 5.1 shows the key differences between the two processes.

**Table 5.1** *Assessment options*

| Activity | Varied timescale option | Three-year option |
| --- | --- | --- |
| Preparation | <ul><li>Complete change pro forma</li><li>Provide organizational chart</li><li>Provide current business plan (including information about training and development and resources)</li></ul> | <ul><li>Provide the same information as for the variable timescale review process</li><li>Provide a storyboard with an updated portfolio</li></ul> |
| On-site review | <ul><li>Planning of assessment with you</li><li>Opportunity to ask questions and provide additional information</li><li>Interviews will focus on the changes made since the previous assessment</li><li>Feedback is provided immediately unless there are exceptional reasons which make this impossible</li><li>Where gaps are identified the Assessor will discuss how long it should take to fill these</li><li>A date for your new review will be established</li><li>The report of the review visit will be sent to you within one week of the visit</li></ul> | <ul><li>Planning of assessment with you</li><li>Opportunity to ask questions and provide additional information</li><li>Interviews will focus on the changes made since the previous assessment</li><li>Feedback is provided after the Recognition Panel meeting</li><li>Where gaps are identified the Assessor will discuss how long it should take to fill these</li><li>A date for your new review will be established</li><li>The report of the review will be provided after the Recognition Panel meeting</li></ul> |
| Feedback | <ul><li>Feedback on how well your company meets the National Standard's requirements will be provided by the Assessor before leaving your premises</li><li>The Assessment report will be written and presented to the assessment unit for verification</li><li>The report will be sent to you one week after the site visit</li><li>A date for the next review visit will be agreed with you at the end of the site visit</li></ul> | <ul><li>Feedback on how well your com pany meets the National Standard's requirements will be provided by the Assessor after the Recognition Panel meeting</li><li>The Assessment report will be written and presented to the Recognition Panel for verification</li><li>The report will be sent to you one week after the Recognition Panel Meeting</li><li>A date for the next review visit will be agreed with you at the end of the site visit</li></ul> |

Table 5.1 captures the main differences between the two approaches to reassessment. Essentially the choice of approach will depend on the type of business you operate. Some issues that you may wish to consider when making these choices are highlighted in the following questions:

- Are your business processes changed frequently?
- Is there a high rate of change in the market you serve?
- Do employee numbers frequently change?
- Does the shape of your business (products, services and employee numbers) change frequently?

If the answer to most of the questions above is yes, then the best option for your company is likely to be the variable timescale review process. If the business remains reasonably static then the three-year cycle is probably most suitable. The local LEC/TEC will provide assistance and a guide for recognized organizations is available from Investors in People UK.

## ILLUSTRATION I

### PIEDA plc

*Submission for assessment against the National Standard Investors in People*

*Date of Assessment November 1995*

*Contents*

*Introduction to the organization*

*Narrative and the evidence*

Commitment
Planning
Action
Evaluation
Appendix I: Details of those interviewed

### INTRODUCTION TO THE ORGANIZATION

*Pieda* plc was established in 1976 as a partnership operating out of offices in Edinburgh. At that time the staff complement consisted of one full-time professional, one secretary and four part-time professors. The current complement is 68, with four offices spread throughout the UK.

*Pieda*'s core business at the time of its inception was economics, planning and development. As the business grew a number of additional functions were added. These functions resulted in the current portfolio of services, which includes bespoke consultancy in the following:

- economics;
- planning and development;
- tourism and leisure;
- housing;
- management consultancy.

The company's four offices are located in Edinburgh, Manchester, Reading and Belfast. The company provides services to the private and public sectors, industry associations and federations.

*Pieda*'s commitment to the Investors in People process in March 1994 reflects the philosophy of the company:

*Our aim is to build a successful business based on professional competence, service quality and customer care.*

### Quotations

*People are not able to fall through holes. There is a higher profile for training and development . . . it's on the agenda now.*
Chairman

*I am the developer for all Directors. We recruit the best person for the post and have several examples of staff moving up . . . one receptionist is now a research manager, another is a senior secretary.*
Chief Executive

*When I joined I had little knowledge of consultancy . . . he's a good teacher, very supportive and a good motivator.*
Economist

*I've never been anywhere where I've felt more comfortable asking questions. It's the best place for looking after new employees. It took me months to settle in (at my last job) but not here.*
Receptionist

## COMMITMENT: THE EVIDENCE

**1.1 The commitment from top management to train and develop employees is communicated effectively throughout the organization.**

There are a number of mechanisms used by the company to ensure that the commitment of senior management is communicated to staff. These mechanisms work together to provide strong evidence of this commitment and include: the chairman's staff conference address, entries in the corporate plan, the induction and appraisal systems and the chairman's six-monthly performance report.

**1.2 Employees at all levels are aware of the broad aims or vision of the organization.**

In conjunction with the processes outlined at 1.1 above, and systems described under indicators 2.3 and 3.1, the company ensures that staff are aware of the aims of the business through the mission statement. This statement is prominently displayed in all offices.

**1.3 The organization has considered what employees at all levels will contribute to the success of the organization, and has communicated this effectively to them.**

There are three main systems used to ensure that staff are aware of the contribution they make to the business. These are: staff appraisal (see 2.3), project management and induction (see 3.1). The project management system provides staff with an opportunity to review their contribution to a particular project and to discuss how this could be improved. This process occurs through the life of a project with a formal review conducted at the end of each activity. Staff who work in the support side of the business are provided with a similar opportunity through the staff developer system. This system is common to all staff and is explained at indicator 2.3.

**1.4 Where representative structures exist, communication takes place between management and representatives on the vision of where the organization is going and the contribution employees (and their representatives) will make to its success.**

No representative structure exists.

## PLANNING: THE EVIDENCE

**2.1 A written but flexible plan sets out the organization's goals and targets.**

Planning is conducted annually with input from local offices and the Board. A corporate plan is produced each year, which captures the local plans and provides a focus for the overall aims and objectives of the business. A three-year corporate plan describes the strategic aims and objectives of the business. It provides the planning framework within which the annual office plans are developed. Local plans are prepared in June and the corporate plan is reviewed and updated in July, for approval by the Board in August.

**2.2 A written plan identifies the organization's training and development needs, and specifies what actions will be taken to meet these needs.**

The corporate and local plans both contain the broad development needs of the company. These needs are expressed as general areas for development and are linked to strategic objectives established through the planning process. In addition, the company operates a training policy to ensure needs are aligned to the business goals. The human resource year runs in parallel to the business planning year and the system to identify needs is well integrated into this process. The plan sets out clearly how the identified needs will be met. The appraisal process is used to assess individual needs and these are fed to a director whose responsibility is to ensure that no non-essential requests are made.

Training and development plans are reviewed against local business plans on a quarterly basis and against the corporate plan annually. A training and development report is submitted to the Board in September of each year. This report is a summary of needs and outcomes assessed against the business objectives.

**2.3 Training and development needs are regularly reviewed against goals and targets at the organization, team and individual level.**

There are two main systems to support the review of staff needs: staff appraisal and project management. These systems are assisted by two additional methods: staff induction (see 3.1) and the staff developer system, which is described below.

The project management system considers the needs of professional staff and is used during and after a project is completed to review the contribution made to a project. Where a skills deficiency is identified this is highlighted for action.

These two systems ensure that the performance of all staff is measured against business requirements and that needs relate to the company's objectives. The developer system provides an additional dimension to the review of staff needs. This system focuses on the long-term needs of staff and establishes a mentoring-type relationship between the developer and the member of staff. Needs identified as a result of the twice yearly meetings with a developer are fed into the appraisal system. Appraisers and developers are not the same people: appraisal is normally the responsibility of the line manager, while the developer is a senior member of staff who does not normally have a direct work relationship with the member of staff.

**2.4 A written plan identifies the resources that will be used to meet training and development needs.**

Considerable resources are used to meet the training and development needs of staff. The company has a nominated training officer in each local office with responsibility for the procurement of training, evaluation of its effectiveness and management of the expenditure against budgets. Staff trainers provide on-the-job training where this is deemed the most appropriate delivery mechanism. Each office has a range of training facilities and all professional staff are now recording the time spent on training and development. The budget for training and development is partly historically based, containing an element of long-term planning for ongoing costs for activities that straddle two or more years.

**2.5 Responsibility for training and developing employees is clearly identified and understood throughout the organization, starting at the top.**

Responsibility for the development of staff is discharged throughout the company. The chief executive, directors and line managers all hold responsibility for development of staff. Project managers are also responsible for the identification of training and development needs.

**2.6 Objectives are set for training and development actions at the organization, team and individual level.**

Targets and standards for development actions are established in either quantitative or qualitative terms, for example participation in three presentations per year or improved report writing skills.

Pre-activity meetings are the norm for development activities and the company uses this method as the main tool in determining the appropriate target or standard for an individual's development. The base line for such discussion is always the highest standard available at that time and stems from the high level of professionalism established by senior managers.

**2.7 Where appropriate, training and development targets are linked to external standards, and particularly to National Vocational Qualifications (NVQs) or Scottish Vocational Qualifications (SVQs) and units.**

A large number of staff are currently pursuing external qualifications ranging from HNC and Btec National courses in accounting and administrative skills to professional courses such as an MSc in Urban and Regional Planning.

### ACTION: THE EVIDENCE

**3.1 All new employees are introduced effectively to the organization and all employees new to a job are given the training and development they need to do that job.**

A comprehensive induction process is well established within the company. Apart from the induction checklist and manual, a godparent is allocated to each new member of staff. This individual is not the new start's line manager, but is likely to work in the same area or type of job as the new member of staff. The godparent is able to provide support and answer any questions that the new employees may have and provides this support for the first three months of employment. Upon completion of the first three months' employment a formal review is conducted with the line manager and staff developer. At this point the new member of staff will have a training and development review and is slotted into the company's appraisal and staff developer systems.

A similar system operates for transferees and promotees, although this is an area that the company recognizes is less well established than the induction for new staff. Key areas of work experience are identified for these individuals for the first three months and a review meeting is held at the end of this period to ensure training and development needs are established. Where promotions have occurred these have been as a result of high levels of competence and as recognition of the capabilities of staff.

The promotion of staff from within is fundamental to the philoso-phy of *Pieda* who are determined to *'grow their own people'*.

**3.2 Managers are effective in carrying out their responsibilities for training and developing employees.**

The appraisal system is used to highlight the competence of man-agers to train and develop staff. Study management: a good practice guide is used to make explicit the requirements of man-agers towards staff development and a number of course-based training activities are currently under way to ensure all managers are competent to undertake these responsibilities. In addition, the experience of managers and formal qualifications held support this indicator.

**3.2 The skills of existing employees are developed in line with business objectives.**

The skills of staff are developed in line with business objectives through the application of the staff developer system, the appraisal process, induction procedures, project post mortems and staff con-ferences.

**3.3 Managers are actively involved in supporting employees to meet their training and development needs.**

The systems described in this report highlight the level of activity that managers are expected to participate in throughout the com-pany's human resource year. These include the staff developer sys-tem, appraisal, project post mortems and day-to-day contact with staff to develop their skills.

**3.4 All employees are made aware of the training and develop-ment opportunities open to them.**

The staff developer system is an effective tool through which devel-opment opportunities for individuals are highlighted. In addition, the staff conference, the chairman's letters, twice yearly staff meet-ings and day-to-day communications ensure that staff are aware of the opportunities open to them. The company operates an Equal Opportunities policy.

**3.5 All employees are encouraged to help identify and meet their job-related development needs.**

Staff are encouraged to take responsibility for their own develop-ment and are supported through the various systems described in this report. Continuing professional development is addressed by staff who are best placed to highlight appropriate developments in their own field of expertise. The staff appraisal process has a separate form, which each person completes prior to the appraisal meeting, highlighting development areas that they feel would be beneficial to the company and to themselves.

**3.6 Action takes place to meet the training and development needs of individuals, teams and the organization.**

A summary of the company's training and development record is presented to the Board at the end of the human resource year. This record confirms that training and development takes place. Interviewees confirmed that where a need has been agreed, action takes place to meet this need.

### EVALUATION: THE EVIDENCE

**4.1 The organization evaluates the impact of training and development actions on knowledge, skills and attitude.**

Individual development actions are evaluated using post-activity audit forms. These forms probe the quality, relevance and impact of courses *vis-à-vis* their objectives. Training officers at each site are responsible for assessing the overall cost-effectiveness of the courses undertaken. At the end of each financial year training officers compile a report which assesses the relevance, effectiveness and value for money of training and development activity. A summary report is presented to the Board in November of each year.

**4.2 The organization evaluates the impact of training and development actions on performance.**

The outcomes of training and development are evaluated at individual, team and organizational levels using the systems described at 2.3, 4.1 and 4.2 in this report. Examples of such evaluation include individuals gaining external qualifications, effective and fast introduction into the company for new starts and a high profile for the company in the business community.

**4.3 The organization evaluates the contribution of training and development to the achievement of its goals and targets.**

The processes used to ensure that relevant training and development takes place include: the local and corporate business planning process, evaluation of training and development report and Board review meetings. The business planning process, at local and corporate levels, evaluates the impact that the previous year's activity has had. The outcome of this evaluation is summarized in the evaluation of training and development report. Quarterly Board meetings have an agenda item that focuses on the effectiveness of training and development activity to ensure a strategic review takes place.

**4.4 Top management understand the broad cost and benefit of training and developing employees.**

Senior managers, and indeed managers at lower levels, were very aware of the costs and benefits associated with training and developing staff.

**4.5 Action takes place to implement improvements to training and development identified as a result of evaluation.**

As each project is reviewed and as a result of appraisal meetings, staff training and development needs are monitored to ensure that the appropriate developments have taken place and have been effective. As results of such developments become clear, the best practices are repeated to provide further strength to the organization and its staff. Where unsuccessful developments have occurred, the reasons for this are considered and amendments made to ensure success in the future. The whole staff and business review process are closely linked to ensure that the evaluation of activity is fed back into the appropriate system.

**4.6 Top management's continuing commitment to training and developing employees is demonstrated to all employees.**

The continuing commitment to train and develop staff is best expressed by quoting an Associate Director:

*Even if we lost all the manuals tomorrow things would continue . . . we have a clear focus on how to identify training and development. Our corporate culture has changed . . . things happen naturally now.*

**APPENDIX I: DETAILS OF THOSE INTERVIEWED**

| POST | M/F | LOS (YRS) |
|---|---|---|
| **Edinburgh** | | |
| Chairman | M | 19 |
| Chief Executive | M | 19 |
| Associate Director | M | 3 |
| Economist | F | 7 |
| Economist | F | 4 |
| Consultant | M | 3 |
| Assistant Consultant | M | 5 mths |
| Receptionist | F | 3 mths |
| Accounts Assistant | F | 3 mths |
| Accountant | M | 5.5 |
| **Reading** | | |
| Senior Consultant | M | 1 |
| Assistant Consultant | F | 3 mths |
| Office Manager | F | 6 |
| Director | M | 9 |
| **Manchester** | | |
| Director | F | 6 |
| Senior Consultant/Training Officer | F | 4 |
| Economist | F | 4 mths |
| Secretary | F | 3 |
| Secretary | F | 2 |

In total 19 employees were interviewed, a sample size of 32 per cent

**ILLUSTRATION II**

**ETHICON LIMITED**

*Submission for assessment against the National Standard Investors in People*

Contents

Introduction to the organization
*Narrative and evidence:*
  Commitment
  Planning

Action
Evaluation
Appendix I:   Details of those interviewed

## INTRODUCTION TO THE ORGANIZATION

Ethicon Limited, Edinburgh (Ethicon) were first recognized as an Investor in People in June 1993. Since then the company has undertaken a number of major changes to the operating structure of the business. At the time of the first assessment traditional, flow line manufacture dominated the operations of the business, with only 10 per cent cell manufacture in place. One of the key aims of the business was to move the remaining 90 per cent of the operations to cell manufacture. At the time of the reassessment, 80 per cent of the factory was operating in cells.

Ethicon Limited, Edinburgh is one of a number of franchised manufacturing plants that operate on behalf of Johnson and Johnson. Within the UK the family of Johnson and Johnson companies is divided into three groups:

- consumer and personal;
- pharmaceutical and diagnostics;
- professional.

The Edinburgh site operates within the professional group with functions comprising:

- research and development;
- manufacturing and hosts the UK headquarters;
- endo-surgery – UK headquarters.

There are 10 other Johnson and Johnson sites throughout the UK. The Edinburgh site is a franchised operation and meets the autonomy guidelines for Investors in People purposes. At the time of the assessment the company employed 1,650 staff.

A number of quality awards have been attained during the period of recognition, including the Johnson and Johnson 'Signature of Quality' Award – bronze level, and the 'Good Laboratory Practice' award from the Department of Health.

The company uses the Johnson and Johnson *Credo* as the basis of its business operations and decision making. This *Credo* is a wide-ranging statement of intent and an expression of how Ethicon will work in business, the community and in its dealings with people.

The recent Dunblane disaster reflects just one example of how the *Credo* is used to uphold the Johnson and Johnson philosophy. A collection was made by Ethicon staff for the Dunblane Appeal and Ethicon offered to double the total; Johnson and Johnson subsequently offered to double that figure.

## COMMITMENT

**1.1 The commitment from top management to train and develop employees is communicated effectively throughout the organization.**

The Johnson and Johnson *Credo* was created over 50 years ago and is still used as the basis of the philosophical approach taken to the development of staff. The *Credo* states:

*We are responsible to our employees . . . everyone must be treated as an individual . . . there must be equal opportunity for employment, development and advancement for those qualified.*

This approach permeates the whole company and is used as a benchmark for the business. Its influence can be seen in the many written documents and operational practices used to support the development of staff. Mission statements, director's briefings and 'customer bonding', where Ethicon has used the Investors in People values to enhance customer satisfaction, reflect the *Credo* and the undoubted value placed upon the company's human capital.

**1.2 Employees at all levels are aware of the broad aims or vision of the organization.**

The company has a mission and a vision statement. These are displayed prominently throughout the company's sites and were clearly understood by interviewees. To ensure that employees are aware of the aims of the business a number of mechanisms are used to provide updated information. For example, the in-house magazine *Tie Line* and the broad-sheet *Quality First* are published bi-monthly. A moving message system relays key items of information received at short notice or where a reminder of a specific issue is required. Quarterly the newsletter *Viewpoint* is distributed to Ethicon's customers and to staff to keep them informed about customer issues.

The briefing systems, which cascade downward from the directors, provide key details on company performance and forward plans. A five-year *Credo* survey measures the effectiveness of the communication processes and a number of cross-functional groups exist to promote effective information flow.

**1.3 The organization has considered what employees at all levels will contribute to the success of the organization, and has communicated this effectively to them.**

Job descriptions exist for every job and these are updated annually or as required. In addition to job descriptions, employees' contribution is measured via the appraisal system and career development plans. At operator level in-house certificated training ensures that staff are aware of the contribution to the success of the business through the quality improvement process; staff are provided with feedback on a weekly basis regarding their work standards and rate of production.

**1.4 Where representative structures exist, communication takes place between management and representatives on the vision of where the organization is going and the contribution employees (and their representatives) will make to its success.**

Ethicon is a non-union company but has a number of representative structures
such as:

- the communications group;
- the rewards group;
- the absence group;
- the health and safety group.

Staff involved with these groups were clear about the methods of communication and the part they played in contributing to the success of the business.

## PLANNING

**2.1 A written but flexible plan sets out the organization's goals and targets.**

A comprehensive business plan exists which details the strategic plan and key objectives for the business. This document sets out the parameters of the business operations and provides a platform for the development of divisional strategies, including the human resource strategy. The company adheres to the Johnson and Johnson quality standards established at an international level and measured through the 'Signature of Quality' award framework.

This award measures key functions such as strategic planning and leadership.

**2.2 A written plan identifies the organization's training and development needs, and specifies what actions will be taken to meet these needs.**

The human resources mission states:

*to help achieve total customer satisfaction by attracting, retaining and developing employees with the skills necessary to meet the strategic needs of internal customers within a safe and healthy working environment.*

This mission is reinforced by the employee development strategy, which has four key objectives. These objectives begin with a focused approach to employee development to ensure customer satisfaction and work through to issues such as the total employee involvement through employee empowerment.

Through the annual business plans for management development, operations and audio-visual the employee development strategy identifies the broad development needs of staff, the methods and cost of delivery.

Each division creates a business plan based upon the strategic plan and key objectives. Within each plan a separate section details the training and development needs of staff to achieve that plan. These needs are reviewed through the performance management system and weekly meetings monitor production, recruitment and operations training. At a senior level the board considers the skills set requirement on an annual basis and establishes development priorities from this. These three separate processes support the review training and development needs against business objectives, thereby ensuring successful succession planning and continuous improvement.

**2.3    Training and development needs are regularly reviewed against goals and targets at the organization, team and individual level.**

The annual performance review system, which has been operational in its present form for approximately nine months, is used to review performance against objectives, the contribution of added value to the business, by the individual and to assess potential for the future. Development needs are then identified to support the objectives that are established, to progress the individual towards achieving these.

The new system provides greater scope for managers to assess staff and gives clear examples of the activities and standards that would achieve a particular rating. The rating system is used by staff to self-assess their performance and to facilitate discussion at the appraisal meeting which takes place with a line manager.

The performance merit system is used for some employees, mostly team leaders, and operates on an annual basis. All production staff are monitored daily with results of outputs fed back on a weekly basis through the 'time-sheets' system. Team leaders monitor results daily and provide training as a result of on-the-job observation.

### 2.4 A written plan identifies the resources that will be used to meet training and development needs.

The annual business plans for each division identify the methods and cost of delivery for training and development. In 1995 an average of two training and development events per employee was recorded and 2.1 per cent of the salary costs was used to fund this activity. The percentage included expenditure on items such as travel, trainers' salaries, training materials, seminars, external courses, books and fees for professional institutions.

Forecasting for the training budget takes place in June of each year and is based on the needs identified at that time. This process ensures that the resources required are set aside for the delivery of this activity.

### 2.5 Responsibility for training and developing employees is clearly identified and understood throughout the organization, starting at the top.

Responsibility to train and develop staff has always been part of the company's *Credo*. Job descriptions make clear these responsibilities and the participation of managers in performance reviews ensures that managers carry out these responsibilities. At Board level the Personnel Director represents staff training and development and is assisted in this by the Johnson and Johnson Corporate Education and Training policy.

### 2.6 Objectives are set for training and development actions at the organization, team and individual level.

The new performance review system is based on setting measurable objectives. Operator training has specific targets for all trainees to reach before being deemed competent and at company-wide level a number of external standards are used to measure activity and to train where gaps are identified. These standards include the *Credo* survey, 'Signature of Quality', ISO9001 and the Good Manufacturing Practice audit.

**2.7 Where appropriate, training and development targets are linked to external standards, and particularly to National Vocational Qualifications (NVQs) or Scottish Vocational Qualifications (SVQs) and units.**

A large number of staff are undertaking externally certificated qualifications ranging from awards from the British Institute of Cleaning through to research degrees and professional qualifications.

## ACTION

**3.1 All new employees are introduced effectively to the organization and all employees new to a job are given the training and development they need to do that job.**

A comprehensive induction process is in place to ensure that all employees are introduced effectively into the company. A company Handbook outlines the main employee relations policies and all staff receive a copy of the *Credo* with their offer letter. Basics such as Health and Safety form part of the induction for all staff and, depending upon job type, a tailor-made induction will be arranged. An orientation programme is used to ensure that staff have a comprehensive knowledge of all aspects of the company's policies, practices and philosophy.

Where staff change jobs line managers deliver on-the-job induction training.

**3.2 Managers are effective in carrying out their responsibilities for training and developing employees.**

The *Credo* states:

*We must provide competent management, and their actions must be just and ethical.*

This statement is translated into reality via the many training and development programmes available to managers and through ongoing development where internal systems change. An example of ongoing support is the new performance review system where briefing sessions were conducted during 1995 and are continued regularly for all appraisees.

To ensure that the manager's competence is at the agreed standard, the Human Resources Director receives completed review documents and advises the appraiser where inconsistencies or incomplete appraisals have been noted. Coaching and counselling skills are being enhanced, as a result of a pilot programme of facilitation training in 1995, for team leaders.

### 3.3 Managers are actively involved in supporting employees to meet their training and development needs.

Employees are encouraged to set their own objectives in conjunction with their line manager and to discuss career aspirations. Teams are also encouraged to identify team developments and monitor progress towards achievements. Where individuals take up the opportunity to study a course of learning, at their own initiative, the company may reimburse course costs where this activity enhances the skills required to do their job.

### 3.4 All employees are made aware of the training and development opportunities open to them.

Development opportunities for staff are discussed at performance review meetings, recruitment interviews, induction and orientation training sessions and on a day-to-day basis through normal contact between line managers and staff. Notice boards and the in-house magazines offer further information on the developments open to staff.

### 3.5 All employees are encouraged to help identify and meet their job-related development needs.

Managers' support to assist employees in identifying their job-related needs takes the form of coaching, mentoring and active involvement in training and development. In addition, managers review performance formally through the annual system which is in place and provide ongoing support throughout the year.

So the skills of employees are monitored through the appraisal system and the operator training programmes and line managers are responsible for ensuring that staff are equipped with the necessary skills to carry out their job effectively.

**3.6 Action takes place to meet the training and development needs of individuals, teams and the organization.**

The company keeps comprehensive computer and paper-based records of all training and development activity and report monthly to the Board via the human resource management group and annually in the employee development report. Where training and development activity has been agreed, this normally takes place. Where agreed activity is not actioned this is as a result of re-prioritization of business needs.

## EVALUATION

**4.1    The organization evaluates the impact of training and development actions on knowledge, skills and attitude.**

Course evaluation forms are completed at the end of each training activity and a three-month follow-up evaluation is completed in conjunction with employees who have participated in training, emphasizing the application of new skills or knowledge. Results are summarized and evaluation information captured at the annual performance review meeting.

**4.2    The organization evaluates the impact of training and development actions on performance.**

The company measures at all three levels required to meet the National Standard's requirements; for example, at an organizational level the Department of Health's Blue Guide (Good Manufacturing Practice) audit assesses the effectiveness of training practice against the ISO9001 standard. This standard is crucial to Ethicon to enable sales of its products in Europe.

At team or group level, evaluation of training and development is monitored in a number of ways; for example, continuous flow manufacture cells have individual targets, which are monitored daily, and weekly graphs show results. The effectiveness of team leader training is measured via the results of individual teams and statistics such as absence rates and labour turnover.

At an individual level, new skills and knowledge or certification of these mark the effective training and development of staff.

**4.3 The organization evaluates the contribution of training and development to the achievement of its goals and targets.**

At a strategic level the company uses a number of short- and long-term measures to capture the effectiveness that training and development of staff has had on the business and targets. Every five years a *Credo* survey is conducted to measure how well staff believe that the values of the *Credo* are being upheld and to monitor changes over time in this perception. The company is also measured against the Johnson and Johnson Signature of Quality award. This award measures key results such as the development and implementation of the business strategy, the utilization of the human resources and the effectiveness of the Education and Training policy. The measures of success for this award are not restricted to a particular group of staff; it covers the whole human capital employed. Log books are kept for assistant technicians and operator training is evaluated against quality standards with graphical representation of results to prove clear outcomes.

Annually an Employee Development Report is produced and breaks down the activity of the training and development function against the strategic vision, employee development goals and objectives and outlines the measures of employee development. This information is further broken down to provide statistical results for training and development, for example the number of training interventions in a particular area over the year. The performance review system completes the package of measures used to evaluate training and development.

**4.4 Top management understand the broad cost and benefit of training and developing employees.**

Department heads complete annual training forecasts with assistance from members of employee development staff thereby ensuring their participation and increased understanding of the costs and benefits of training and developing staff.

**4.5 Action takes place to implement improvements to training and development identified as a result of evaluation.**

The evaluation processes used by the company have improved as a result of the first assessment and will continue to improve as the new appraisal system becomes fully implemented.

**4.6 Top management's continuing commitment to training and developing employees is demonstrated to all employees.**

The company has taken the philosophy of Investors in People and used it, not only to their own advantage, but to the advantage of the community it serves. Ethicon has provided and continues to provide customers with information on the Investors in People Standard and uses these principles to assist individual communities within the Edinburgh area. The continued commitment to the National Standard is strong.

**APPENDIX I: DETAILS OF THOSE INTERVIEWED**

Interview schedule, Ethicon Limited

| POST | M/F | LOS (YRS) |
|---|---|---|
| **25 March 1996, Assessor: Mary McLuskey** | | |
| **Sighthill** | | |
| Managing Director | M | 9 mths |
| Machine Operators (4) | F | 2–16 |
| Team Leaders (3) | M | 10, 4 mths, 11 mths |
| Sales Consultant | F | 2 |
| Quality Compliance Mgr | M | 3 |
| International Shipping Mgr | F | 10 |
| Lab Technician | F | 11.5 |
| CFM Prol Operators (3) | F | 2–16 |
| Kirkton Campus | | |
| CFM Operators (4) | F (x3), M (1) | 2–3 |
| Manager of Management Development | F | 4 |
| **25 March 1996, Assessor: Bill Collie** | | |
| **Sighthill** | | |
| Human Resources Director | M | |
| International Sales Director | M | |
| Manager of Operations, Training | F | |
| Instructors (2) | F | |
| Class 'A' Attachers (3) | F | |
| QA Inspectors (3) | F | |
| CFM Operators (4) | M (x3, M (x1) | |
| Cell Group Leader (2) | M, F | |

| POST | M/F | LOS (YRS) |
|---|---|---|
| **26 March 1996, Assessor: Bill Collie** | | |
| **Fountain Bridge** | | |
| Winders (3) | F | |
| Premium Inspectors (4) | F | |
| **Sighthill** | | |
| Machine Operators (4) | F (2), M (2) | |
| Director | M | |
| Secretaries (4) | F | |
| Plant Engineer | M | |
| Assistant Technician | M | |
| Engineer Leading Hand | M | |
| Security Guard | M | |
| Housekeeping (3) | M (2), F | |
| Suture Packers (3) | M (2), F | |
| Distribution Operators (2) | M, F | |

In total 69 employees were interviewed, a sample size of 4.2 per cent.

## Summary

Remember that proper preparation for the assessment is extremely important. To assist you in preparation the following exercise will help you to focus on those activities that need to be conducted to make the assessment process painless.

The key aspects that you must address when producing your story-board and portfolio are the following:

- Provide a brief introduction to your business, its background, products and markets.
- Give clear information about your employees, how many people you employ, the jobs they do, and if possible, their length of service.
- Describe the processes or systems that are in place to meet each part of the National Standard. This book shows you how several companies have done this and will assist you in gathering your own information.
- Include an organizational chart, if you have one, or describe the structure of the company.

- Use a matrix of written evidence to represent the evidence you are presenting. This has two purposes; first, it ensures that you have checked that you are able to present information against each indicator to support your application for recognition, and second, it will assist the Assessor in finding the way through your portfolio of evidence.
- Keep the amount of evidence to a minimum: normally one or two items of evidence are sufficient to support each indicator.

## Exercise 5.2

1. Using the blank matrix at the back of this book, list in the first column those documents that currently exist within your company that you feel could be used to support your application for assessment.
2. Consider each document listed and, taking each in turn, tick the boxes under each of the indicators that you feel the document supports.
3. After completing this for each document listed, check to see if there are any indicators that have no ticks or are weak. If so, note these indicators and consider:
   (i) Have you omitted any documentation that would support the gaps?
   (ii) If no documentation exists, have you described the process(es) used in your company at the appropriate part of your storyboard?
   (iii) Do you need to develop a new process to fill this gap?

It may be helpful, while conducting this exercise, to refer back to the illustrations presented throughout this book and to make use of the exercises that you have completed at the end of each of the first four chapters.

# ◀ CHAPTER 6 ▶

# LINKS TO THE EUROPEAN FOUNDATION FOR QUALITY MANAGEMENT EXCELLENCE MODEL

*500 staff meetings, 30 lawyers, 25 civil servants, 6 managerial briefings, 3 Queen's Counsel, 2 Secretaries of State, 1 Act of Parliament and 4 months later, I have come to realize that it wasn't as simple as I thought.*

Peter Thompson, Chairman, *NFC Ltd (The National Freight Buy Out: The Inside Story)*

### Outline of the European Foundation for Quality Management Excellence Model

**Comprehensive coverage of all business processes**

The European Quality Award was presented for the first time in 1992. The European Organization for Quality and the European Commission took the lead in establishing the European Quality Award, which is given to the most successful exponent of Total Quality Management in Europe. The model is currently based on nine elements, which provide comprehensive coverage of all business processes, and systems through which an organization can plan, implement, monitor and improve.

The nine elements are shown below:

- Leadership (100 points)

- Policy and strategy (80 points)
- People (90 points)
- Partnership and Resources (90 points)
- Processes (140 points)
- Customer results (200 points)
- People results (90 points)
- Society results (60 points)
- Key performance results. (150 points)

The model is based on a system of scoring each of these elements with a maximum score of 1,000 points available. These points are divided between the nine elements as shown in the brackets above. There are two categories of elements within the model: these are Enablers and Results. Enablers are those elements that deal with how the organization approaches this part of the model. Results are therefore concerned with what the organization has achieved. When scoring the Enablers, account must be taken of the approach that has been adopted and how well the approach is deployed across the whole organization. So an effective approach may score well but the total score may be reduced if the deployment of this approach is not applied consistently.

**Enablers and results**

   As an example:

## 1(a)  Leadership

How leaders develop and facilitate the achievement of the mission and vision, develop values required for long-term success and implement these via appropriate actions and behaviours, and are personally involved in ensuring that the organization's management system is developed and implemented.

A score of 60 is given for the approach and a score of 40 for deployment. This scoring would reflect that for this criterion in the Leadership element an effective approach has been developed but it is only being deployed, or used, to about 40 per cent per cent of its potential within the whole organization. To find the actual score for this criterion, a simple arithmetic average of the approach and deployment scores is taken. This gives a score for criterion 1(a) of 50:

$$60 + 40 = 100 \div 2 = 50$$

This scoring method is applied to all Enablers until each element is complete. The next step is to find the arithmetic average of each element. For example:

**1. Leadership**

**Criterion Part   1 (a) 50**

**1 (b) 45**

**1 (c) 60**

**1 (d) 65**

**220 ÷ 4 = 55**

So, for the Enabler, Leadership, the score awarded would be 55.

This scoring process is repeated for each of the five Enablers and their corresponding criterion parts, of which there are 24 in total. To find the value of the points of each Enabler the individual scores are multiplied by a percentage factor or weighting. The weighting corresponds to the overall importance of each element within the whole Excellence Model. See Figure 6.1.

**Table 6.1** *EFQM Enablers scores*

| Enabler | Score Factor | Points |
|---|---|---|
| 1.  Leadership | 55 × 1.0 | 55 |
| 2.  Policy and Strategy | 60 × 0.8 | 48 |
| 3.  People | 65 × 0.9 | 58 |
| 4.  Partnerships and Resources | 60 × 0.9 | 54 |
| 5.  Processes | 50 × 1.4 | 70 |
| | **Total** | **285** |

In Table 6.1 the total points awarded for the Enablers part of the model is 285 out of a possible 500.

Scoring Results is basically the same process. The main difference with Results is that the first consideration is how good the actual Result is and then the scope, or how well the Results have affected all areas of the organization and its activities.

For example, Element 6 (a) Customer Results might score 65 for results, reflecting strong trends and excellent performance over a period of three or more years, but the scope might only score 45. The lower score for scope shows that the results may address many relevant areas and activities, but not all.

Again, the arithmetic average of the two scores is taken to obtain the actual score. So in the example, 6 (a) Customer Results scores 55:

**65 + 45 = 110 ÷ 2 = 55**

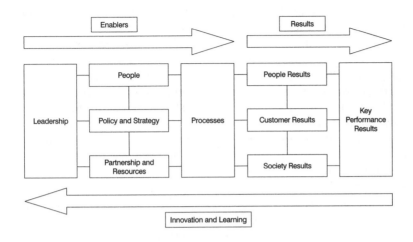

**Figure 6.1** Excellence Model © EFQM

To find the points for Customer Results the score is multiplied by the appropriate factor weighting. In this instance:

**55 × 2.0 = 110**

This process is repeated for all Results to get the points awarded (Table 6.2).

**Table 6.2**

| Result | Score Factor | Points |
| --- | --- | --- |
| 6 Customer Results | 55 × 2.0 | 110 |
| 7 People Results | 70 × 0.9 | 63 |
| 8 Society Results | 60 × 0.6 | 36 |
| 9 Key Performance Results | 62 × 1.5 | 93 |
| | **Total** | **302** |

So the points awarded for the Results part of the model is 302 out of a total available of 500. The total points awarded in this example are shown in Table 6.3.

**Table 6.3**

| | |
| --- | --- |
| Enablers | 285 |
| Results | 302 |
| **Total** | **587** |

**Gap to excellence**

The organization in the example would have scored 587 points out of a total of 1,000, making it a very good example of an excellent organization. The gap between the actual points awarded and those available reflect that there is, however, room for improvement. It is this 'gap to excellence' that facilitates the continuous improvement cycle for organizations that adopt the Excellence Model approach.

The scoring process outlined above should not be undertaken once only. Indeed the strength of the Excellence Model approach is in repeated applications of this scoring process. Taking a score every year will allow organizations to track their progress and ensure that continuous improvement is achieved. However, it is worth mentioning that the first time an organization undertakes the scoring process there are two distinct outcomes that might occur. Over-scoring across the model is common in the early days of its usage. When an organization begins to make use of the model there is a steep learning curve for individuals applying the model. It is inevitable that the reality of an organization's position relative to the model will be either under- or over-scored as a result of lack of understanding. The likelihood is that individuals will adjust their scoring over time as they gain experience of the model and its application.

A critical factor in the scoring system, whether it is for an Award application or whether the model is being used as a tool for continuous improvement within an organization, is that of consensus. For the diagram of the model and the examples given to show how the model works, it is clear that the complexity of application cannot, and indeed should not, be the domain of one individual. To work well the model needs to be applied across the organization, or those parts of the organization that have chosen to adopt it, and should be based on gaining a consensus from the people applying it. Ultimately the team aims to agree a score for the whole model. One method of gaining consensus is to have each leader of a particular element reach an individual score for the whole model and then to meet and discuss their findings. Through discussion, a consensus is achieved by allowing each member the opportunity to state his or her score and provide the rationale for having reached his or her decision.

**Consensus**

In the consensus meeting it is possible to gain consensus by looking at the scores that are at the extremes of the team's average. For example, if a team has scored an element at, say, 65, with one member of the team scoring 30 and another 90, these two individuals need to provide a clear rationale for their choices. Frequently in the discussion that follows it becomes clear that individuals are either too hard or soft in their scoring and have simply overlooked some evidence, or have attributed too much importance to a particular item of evidence. It may be that individuals' understanding of the model's requirements differ because of their own background and knowledge. Whatever the reason, it is important that those individuals who are scoring are capable of presenting their rationale and defending this in the consensus meeting. After debate it may be that the highest and lowest scores are adjusted to find a consensus. Where it is impossible for either person to adjust their score, the team leader must make a final decision about the score, based on the information provided by all members of the team. Eventually a consensus is gained and a score reached. Of vital importance is that the team agrees the areas for improvement, as it is these aspects of the scoring procedure that will provide an action plan for future improvements in the organization.

The Excellence Model is a non-prescriptive framework that aims to engender a culture of continuous improvement where innovation and creativity is actively encouraged. The framework for the model allows for a variety of approaches. The framework provides a generic route map through which organizations can move to sustainable organizational excellence. The model is underpinned by some basic concepts, including the need for appropriate behaviours, attitudes and skills. It is these fundamental concepts that make the Excellence Model an excellent fit with the National Standard Investors in People.

**Non-prescriptive**

Investors in People requires that the attitudes, behaviours and skills of all employees be developed in line with the organization's goals. The Excellence Model also requires this approach and states this explicitly in the sub-criteria for each element, particularly in Leadership and in People. The sub-criteria listed under each of the nine elements provide a guide to the user on how to interpret each element, but are not meant to be followed blindly. By providing such guidance the model can be adapted for use in any organizational environment. Detailed information about the model can be obtained from a number of sources in the UK and Brussels (see section Useful Addresses).

## How Investors in People links to the Excellence Model

Often when an organization recognizes the need for improvement the range of tools and techniques available can be confusing. It is possible to begin a process of change management without giving thought to the end result. The concept of beginning with the end in mind is a useful way of focusing on what needs to be done and how this might be achieved. Clearly there is a need to consider the timescale required

**Tools and techniques**

and the resource implications of any particular approach. For this reason the fit between approaches needs to be considered carefully. Research by Investors in People UK shows that organizations can achieve the National Standard within a period of approximately 18 months to two years. This research shows that small organizations can move more quickly towards achieving the National Standard, but even in larger organizations the timescale does not increase substantially. The Excellence Model approach takes longer, and it is accepted that achievement of this standard can take between three and five years.

**Continuous improvement**

However, both approaches aim at a process of continuous improvement so, in many respects, the timescale for achieving either is less important than the structured methodology each offers to improve organizational processes and results constantly.

Work by a number of bodies[1] including The Cabinet Office, has shown that the linkages between the National Standard Investors in People and the European Foundation for Quality Management Excellence Model are strong and that by undertaking one, the other becomes achievable, if not inevitable (Figure 6.2).

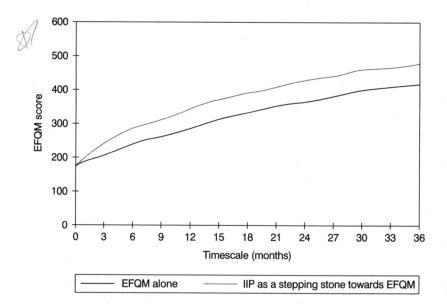

**Figure 6.2** *Progress towards best value. Source: Gerry Farrell, Investors in People Assessor, COSLA*

1 Investors in People UK, Investors in People Scotland, COSLA, Quality Scotland Foundation

## Moving towards excellence

Investors in People requires that standards of good practice are put in place to achieve organizational effectiveness and efficiency. The focus is on integrating the strategic management of people within the organization to achieve performance results. In the Excellence Model approach key performance results take on this role; however, the focus is the same: integration of practices across the whole organization to achieve the high quality outcomes. In both cases the focus is on improvement and on striving for improvements in all aspects of the organization's products or services.

Excellence is something that is hard to define and is perhaps achievable only for short periods. Key to the notion of excellence is that continuous improvement is required to maintain or gain a lead in the market or in provision of services. So, fundamental to the Excellence Model approach is the search for improvement regardless of the level of previous achievements. It is this aspect of 'stretch' that makes the fit between the two models such an attractive one.

One of the main differences between Investors in People and the Excellence Model approach is that the financial aspects of organizational development are fully considered so that people, processes and financial improvements must be achieved before an organization can be considered as having met the requirements of the Excellence Model. There are other differences and these are shown in the following sections.

**Key performance results**

## Self-assessment

As an organizational development tool the Excellence Model approach is very user friendly. Although designed as an Award, the model and its application are primarily aimed at improving organizations through self-directed improvements and self-monitored achievements. External assessment is possible if required; however, there is no need to take this step unless this external endorsement is sought.

Approaches to self-assessment will vary according to the needs of each organization. In many instances a team of individuals from across the organization will come together to form a working group. The team will typically appoint to each individual ownership of a particular element so that all of the component parts of the model are fully considered when making judgements about improvements and progress towards excellence. The team is not working alone. Each person with responsibility for an element will be supported by a group of

**Approaches to self-assessment**

**Approach and deployment**

employees drawn from the whole organization whose work will feed into this main group. By using a self-scoring process each team will be able to assess improvements made and identify areas for further development. It is these areas for further development that make up the continuous improvement cycle. For example, the team with responsibility for the element Leadership may have scored the organization with 40 points out of the 100 available. This leaves room for improvement of 60 points if the approach and deployment of all aspects of the organization's leadership activity are to be considered fully integrated into normal operations and are applied to their full potential.

Using a self-assessment tool can assist the team to determine which aspects of the organization's leadership activity need to improve. So, using the model, the element and the corresponding sub-criteria need to be revisited to identify areas for improvement. In the example above, a score of 40 has been given, so the team needs to look at each part of leadership and determine what can be improved.

The Excellence Model definition of leadership falls into four main headings, the first of which is shown below. Leadership is broadly defined in the Excellence Model as:

**1. Leadership   How leaders develop and facilitate the achievement of the mission and vision, develop values required for long-term success and implement these via appropriate actions and behaviours, and are personally involved in ensuring that the organization's management system is developed and implemented.**

1a. Leaders develop the mission, vision and values and are role models of a culture of Excellence.

Areas to address *could* include *how* leaders:

- develop clear values and expectations for the organization;
- act as role models for the organization's values and expectations, leading by example;
- give and receive training;
- make themselves accessible, listen and respond to the organization's people;
- are active and personally involved in improvement activities;
- review and improve the effectiveness of their own leadership.

| Scores Elements of approach | 0% | 5 | 10 | 15 | 20 | 25% | 30 | 35 | 40 | 45 | 50% | 55 | 60 | 65 | 70 | 75% | 80 | 85 | 90 | 95 | 100% |
|---|---|---|---|---|---|---|---|---|---|---|---|---|---|---|---|---|---|---|---|---|---|
| Soundly based approach | No evidence or anecdotal | | | Some evidence | | | | | X Evidence | | | | | Clear evidence | | | | | Comprehensive evidence | | |
| Systematic and where appropriate preventative | No evidence or anecdotal | | | Some evidence | | | | X | Evidence | | | | | Clear evidence | | | | | Comprehensive evidence | | |
| Review | No evidence or anecdotal | | | Occasional review X | | | | | Regular review with respect to business effectiveness | | | | | Clear evidence of regular review with respect to business effectiveness | | | | | Clear evidence of refinement and improved business effectiveness through review cycles | | |
| Integration | No evidence or anecdotal | | | Some evidence of integration into normal operations | | | | | Evidence of integration into normal operations | | | | X | Clear evidence of integration into normal operations | | | | | Approach is totally integrated into normal operations. Role model | | |

| Approach score | 0% | 5 | 10 | 15 | 20 | 25% | 30 | 35 | 40 | 45 | 50% | 55 | 60 | 65 | 70 | 75% | 80 | 85 | 90 | 95 | 100% |
|---|---|---|---|---|---|---|---|---|---|---|---|---|---|---|---|---|---|---|---|---|---|

| Deployment considering all relevant areas and activities | 0% | 5 | 10 | 15 | 20 | 25% | 30 | 35 | 40 | 45 | 50% | 55 | 60 | 65 | 70 | 75% | 80 | 85 | 90 | 95 | 100% |
|---|---|---|---|---|---|---|---|---|---|---|---|---|---|---|---|---|---|---|---|---|---|
| | Little effective usage | | | Applied to about 1/4 of the potential | | | | | Applied to about 1/2 of the potential | | | | X | Applied to about 3/4 of the potential | | | | | Applied to full potential | | |

| Deployment score | 0% | 5 | 10 | 15 | 20 | 25% | 30 | 35 | 40 | 45 | 50% | 55 | 60 | 65 | 70 | 75% | 80 | 85 | 90 | 95 | 100% |
|---|---|---|---|---|---|---|---|---|---|---|---|---|---|---|---|---|---|---|---|---|---|
| | | | | | | | | | X | | | | | | | | | | | | |

| OVERALL SCORE | 0% | 5 | 10 | 15 | 20 | 25% | 30 | 35 | 40 | 45 | 50% | 55 | 60 | 65 | 70 | 75% | 80 | 85 | 90 | 95 | 100% |
|---|---|---|---|---|---|---|---|---|---|---|---|---|---|---|---|---|---|---|---|---|---|

**Figure 6.3** *EFQM scoring grid*

The team, having scored leadership at 40 (as shown in Figure 6.3), then lists those aspects of the organization's activities that they believe support this score under Strengths, Areas for Improvement and Issues to Clarify. (In a formal assessment this last item would be referred to as Site Visit Issues.)

So, continuing the example, the team identify these aspects as:

1a.   Strengths

- A senior-level corporate steering committee, including the managing director, meets frequently and has established a vision, mission and set of values for the whole organization.
- Senior leaders (30 people) have received quality education over a number of years.
- Senior leaders have devoted 20 per cent of their time to quality initiatives and activities in the past year.
- Senior leaders evaluate their own leadership styles and effectiveness through annual employee surveys, self-assessment appraisals and individual performance appraisals.
- Senior leaders and other leaders are systematically involved in decisions about new products and services.

1a.   Areas for Improvement

- The mission, values and vision focus on the external customer's requirements and do not appear to provide a clear link to other groups, for example employees, society or suppliers.
- Information about a limited number of leaders is given. The extent to which all other leaders are involved in promoting a quality culture is unclear.
- · Little evidence of the involvement of leaders in the delivery of training and how accessible managers are to employees.
- The effectiveness of appraisals and employee surveys is not evaluated.

1a.   Issues to Clarify (Site Visit Issues)

- Are the behaviours of leaders fully addressed in the employee surveys and self-administered appraisals? How do the results of these evaluation tools link to leader's appraisals to inform development actions?

- Clarify how leaders (other than the top 30) contribute to a quality culture.

The results of the assessment by the leadership team are fed into the meeting where all aspects of the model are considered. Each individual with responsibility for an element provides an overview of the results that have been obtained through their own team's self-assessment of the whole organization. Together the team considers the results and agreement is reached on the scores and crucially on the developments that are needed to improve the organization's effectiveness. This process is repeated on a frequent basis so that trends in developments and improvements can be tracked. Over a period of months and years the organization is able to show clear evidence of continuous improvement in all aspects of the model's requirements.

When an organization considers that its score is moving towards excellence, that is, its score is moving into the upper quartile of 65 per cent–100 per cent, it may choose to apply for an Excellence Model Award. This process will require a full submission of how the organization believes it meets the requirements of the model, with details of the methods used within the organization to achieve continuous improvement. Assessment is conducted by qualified assessors who work in teams in much the same way as described in the self-assessment process above.

## Working together: how both models link

Earlier, the links between the National Standard Investors in People and the Excellence Model were shown. In this section these links are described more fully.

One of the key strengths of the Excellence Model approach is the ability of the model to accommodate a range of other approaches. It is non-prescriptive in its application and is able to embrace a wide range of other techniques that organizations select as best fit for their own environment. Figure 6.4 shows how some of the current approaches to developing organizations can fit within the Excellence Model approach. From this diagram it is clear that a wide range of approaches can be used in support of organizational improvement, and the links between Investors in People and the Excellence Model are obvious.

**Best fit with organization's practices**

Correlation between the Excellence Model and the Investors in People indicators (1997)

| Excellence Model Criteria | | Investor in People indicators | | | | | | | | | | | | | | | | | | | | | | | |
|---|---|---|---|---|---|---|---|---|---|---|---|---|---|---|---|---|---|---|---|---|---|---|---|---|---|
| | | 1. Commitment | | | | 2. Planning | | | | | | | 3. Action | | | | | | 4. Evaluation | | | | | |
| | | 1.1 | 1.2 | 1.3 | 1.4 | 2.1 | 2.2 | 2.3 | 2.4 | 2.5 | 2.6 | 2.7 | 3.1 | 3.2 | 3.3 | 3.4 | 3.5 | 3.6 | 4.1 | 4.2 | 4.3 | 4.4 | 4.5 | 4.6 |
| Leadership | 1a | ● | ● | ● | ● | | | | | ● | | | | ● | ● | ● | | | | | | ● | | ● |
| | 1b | ● | | | | | ● | | ● | | | | | | | | | | | | | | | |
| | 1c | | | | | | | | | | | | | | | | | | | | | | | ● |
| | 1d | | | ● | | | | | | | | | | | | | | | | | | | | |
| Policy and Strategy | 2a | | | | ● | | ● | | | | | | | | | | | | | | | | | |
| | 2b | | | | | | | | | | | | | | | | | | | | | | | |
| | 2c | | ● | ● | | ● | | | | | | | | | | | | | | | | | | |
| | 2e | ● | ● | ● | ● | ● | | ● | | | | | ● | | | ● | | ● | ● | | | | | ● |
| People | 3a | | | | | ● | ● | ● | ● | | | | ● | | | | | | ● | ● | ● | ● | ● | |
| | 3b | | ● | ● | | | | ● | ● | | | | ● | | | ● | ● | ● | | ● | ● | | | |
| | 3c | | | | | | | ● | | | | | | | ● | | | | | | | | | |
| | 3d | | | | | | | | | | | | | | | | | | | | | | | |
| | 3e | | | ● | | | | | | | | | | | | | | | | | | | | ● |
| Partnership and Resources | 4a | | | | | | | | ● | | | | | | | | | | | | | | | |
| | 4b | | | | | | | | | | | | | | | | ● | | | | | ● | | |
| | 4c | | | | | | | | | | | | | | | | | | | | | | | |
| | 4d | | | | | | ● | | | | | | | | | | | | | | | | | |
| | 4e | | | | | | ● | ● | | | | | | | | | | | | | | | | |
| Processes | 5a | | | | | | | | | | | | | | | | | | | | | | | |
| | 5b | | | | | | | | | | | | | | | | | | ● | ● | | | | |
| | 5c | | | | | | | | | | | | | | | | | | | | ● | | | |
| | 5d | | | | | | ● | | | | | | | | | | | | | | | | | |
| | 5e | | | | | | | ● | | | | | | | | | | | ● | ● | ● | | ● | |

**Figure 6.4** *Linkages*

Investor in People indicators

| Excellence Model Criteria | | 1. Commitment | | | | 2. Planning | | | | | | | 3. Action | | | | | | 4. Evaluation | | | | | |
|---|---|---|---|---|---|---|---|---|---|---|---|---|---|---|---|---|---|---|---|---|---|---|---|---|
| | | 1.1 | 1.2 | 1.3 | 1.4 | 2.1 | 2.2 | 2.3 | 2.4 | 2.5 | 2.6 | 2.7 | 3.1 | 3.2 | 3.3 | 3.4 | 3.5 | 3.6 | 4.1 | 4.2 | 4.3 | 4.4 | 4.5 | 4.6 |
| Customer | 6a | | ● | ● | | ● | | | | ● | ● | | ● | | | | ● | | | | | | | |
| Results | 6b | | | ● | | ● | | | | ● | ● | | ● | | | | ● | | | | | | | |
| People Results | 7a | ● | ● | ● | | ● | ● | ● | ● | ● | ● | ● | ● | ● | ● | ● | ● | ● | ● | ● | ● | ● | ● | ● |
| | 7b | ● | ● | ● | | ● | ● | ● | ● | ● | ● | ● | ● | ● | ● | ● | ● | ● | ● | ● | ● | ● | ● | ● |
| Society Results | 8a | ● | | | | | | | | | | | | | | ● | | | | | | | | |
| | 8b | ● | | | | | | | | | | | | | | ● | | | | | | | | |
| Key Performance Results | 9a | | | | | ● | | | | | | | | | | | | | ● | | | | | |
| | 9b | | | | | | ● | | | | | | | | | | | | | | ● | | | |

Figure 6.4 *continued*

Investors in People can assist in attaining business excellence through:

- structured and sound approaches to the alignment of people's skills, knowledge and behaviours to the organization's desired business goals and results;
- providing an evaluation cycle that focuses on the main resource differential available to any organization: that is, its people;
- enabling an organization to create a strategic framework for establishing organizational aims, objectives and vision for the future;
- creating a culture of continuous improvement that focuses on the development of employees to achieve business results;
- ensuring that there is equality of development across the organization while striving for incremental and step changes in methods of working;
- providing a mechanism that ensures that employees are not alienated from the organization's mission and aims.

## Continuous improvement

The concept of continuous improvement is not new. For centuries people have striven to improve every aspect of their lives. The translation of this idea into the business world has been a natural progression of the individual's desire to create a better lifestyle. However, the application of a continuous improvement culture in the context of work is not easy. The motivation for improvement has to be understood and barriers to improvements identified, addressed and removed. Individuals' motivation needs to be addressed and channelled towards organizational goals if overall improvements are to be meaningful. As a result, many models for improvement have been designed to increase the results of individuals, teams and whole organizations. What is critical to success is the integration of these approaches to ensure that no one approach works against another to undermine or weaken its application.

**Motivation for improvement**

It is essential that any new approach is tested for robustness, suitability, and cost-effectiveness before a full-scale implementation is begun. In this way, approaches that may not produce the desired effect can be weeded out, saving time and money and preventing disillusionment among the employees who will be affected by the changes required. The illustrations below show how The Scottish Office approached the implementation of the Excellence Model and how piloting provided an ideal mechanism to ensure smooth implementation of the model across a range of departments.

## ILLUSTRATION

### The Scottish Office case study

In August 1997, The Scottish Office, now the Scottish Executive, was recognized as an Investor in People. It was the first government department to be assessed and recognized as a whole organization.

### BACKGROUND TO THE DEPARTMENT

At that time, The Scottish Office was the umbrella title for five main Departments:

- Agriculture, Environment and Fisheries Department;
- Development Department;
- Education and Industry Department;
- Department of Health;
- Home Department.

There was a sixth grouping called Central Services. Their Investors in People assessment also covered their Executive Agencies (excluding the Scottish Prison Service), General Records and the then Scottish Records Office.

The then Scottish Office was a multifunctional government department with responsibility for most aspects of government policy in Scotland other than employment, social security, taxation and defence. Their aim was significant improvement in economic, social and environmental conditions in Scotland.

Their headquarters are in Edinburgh but they also have a large office in Glasgow and smaller offices elsewhere in the country. They have an office in London's Whitehall, to maintain day-to-day liaison with the Westminster parliament and other government departments.

### Why commit to Investors in People?

When Investors in People was launched in 1991, The Scottish Office and the then Department of Employment were the only two government departments to sign up. The Scottish Office made a commitment to become a recognized Investor in People for a number of reasons:

- They believed Investors in People would give them the kind of training and development framework they wanted.
- It was a way of demonstrating top management commitment to training and development.
- The Scottish Office had a policy responsibility for Investors in People in Scotland and they wanted to be able to set a good example.

**Working towards assessment**

Unlike other government departments, The Scottish Office decided that they would approach Investors in People as a whole organization, rather than breaking themselves down into five main departments, their related agencies and Central Services. However, they believed it was the right approach because it tied in with their plans to change the culture of the organization to one that was more flexible, less hierarchical and that encourages people to take more responsibility.

When they self-assessed against the standard they believed they were already doing about 80 per cent per cent of what the standard required. They knew they would have to work hard at the other 20 per cent but they thought it was achievable.

Unlike some other organizations, they took a very low-key approach to Investors in People. An Investors in People label was not attached to the changes that they were making in the Department. The standard was used as a guideline when replacing those systems that needed replacing and to adjust those that needed adjusting.

**The Scottish Office's approach to preparation**

Early in 1992 a staff survey was carried out. It dealt with all aspects of personnel (recruitment, promotion, appraisal, etc). The results overall were less encouraging than anticipated. One outcome of the survey was a major project to restructure the Personnel Division into a much more customer-focused organization. The length of time involved in analysing the survey and completing the subsequent restructuring programme were major factors in the process and the time it took to achieve the National Standard's requirements.

This first survey provided a base from which to begin the changes necessary; however, it also identified some challenges. By 1995, when a second staff survey was carried out, this proved to be a much more focused exercise, identifying three main areas of weakness:

- Members of staff were still having difficulty describing what their department did and even more difficulty describing what the aims of The Scottish Office were.
- Induction processes weren't as good as they might be – especially for staff who were moving jobs within the organization.
- Like many organizations, more work needed to be done on evaluation, particularly on the identification of the impact of training and development on business success.

These shortcomings were addressed by the Management Group, comprising the Permanent Secretary and the Heads of the five departments. A decision to submit an application for formal assessment was then taken with a target of 31 December 1996 for plugging the gaps to match the Standard.

**The assessment process**
Although The Scottish Office had adopted a whole organization approach towards assessment they decided that each department should be assessed in turn. This had two main advantages: it encouraged ownership amongst senior managers; and each department received a separate report which helped to identify problem areas more accurately and therefore target support for continuous improvement to specific areas after the assessment was complete.

There were downsides to this approach. The Assessor had to increase the number of staff she interviewed, and the assessment took longer and was therefore more expensive. The main benefit was that all employees would be aware of, if not involved in, the assessment and that managers would have externally validated data that would highlight areas of good practice and areas for improvement.

**Ownership**
At the start of the process the Head of Training and Development realized that getting the commitment of line managers was crucial

to the success of the process. With the backing of the Permanent Secretary and the Heads of the five departments, an Investors in People Liaison Group, made up of senior managers from each department, was established. The remit of the group was:

- to advise the Head of Training and Development on how aware-ness of Investors in People might be cascaded throughout The Scottish Office;
- to play an appropriate role in that cascading of information;
- to help to identify evidence for the assessment and help to resolve any difficulties in their department; and
- (most crucially) to provide a link between the Investors in People project team and the senior management teams in each of the five departments.

Most of what was required to be done to achieve Investors in People status needed to be done by managers and staff in the line. The project team were under no illusions. They knew that they alone couldn't 'get IiP' for the organization. The Investors in People Liaison Group, because of their understanding of the issues involved and their influential positions in their departments, played an important part in The Scottish Office's success.

**The portfolio**
The Scottish Office portfolio of evidence had been evolving over the years. Advice had been sought from various sources about what evidence to present and how to present it. The Assessor reviewed the portfolio during May and June 1996. She found that all the evidence matched and in some cases exceeded the stan-dard. With hindsight it was clear that the main weakness of the portfolio was of 'talking up' the evidence. By presenting the Assessor with the best of best practice from across the organization they had created very high expectations in the mind of the Assessor and thereby created a problem when it came to the assessment interviews. The matrix of evidence used in the portfo-lio is shown on pages 147–48.

**The interviews**
From June to November 1996 the assessment team interviewed 345 staff in a diverse range of grades and occupational groups, in a

range of locations. Interviews were conducted one-to-one or in small groups.

The majority of these interviews were conducted face-to-face but some were conducted over the telephone for those staff in remote locations. It became clear after the interviews in the first two or three departments that it was unlikely that The Scottish Office would fully meet the standard at that time.

There were a number of reasons for this. Some of the systems and processes described in the portfolio were new and had not had time to go through a full cycle or to 'bed in'. Assessors also found that although there was some extremely good practice there was inconsistency across the whole organization.

**Deferral**

Once it was confirmed that The Scottish Office did not match the standard, they were faced with three options:

- Ignore the Assessor's view and present their case to the Recognition Panel. (They dismissed this option immediately.)
- Ask the Assessor to come back within six months to view additional evidence and conduct more interviews to check whether they had 'plugged the gaps'. In other words, defer assessment.
- Stop the assessment and ask the Assessor to come back and go through the whole process again when they felt that they were ready.

The second option was considered to be best although it was also the most challenging because of further staff cuts, an election and the possibility of a new administration, which, as we know, actually happened. Nevertheless, over the six months between January and June 1997, senior management took the feedback seriously and a tremendous amount of work was done to address the issues that had been highlighted as gaps in the Assessor's reports.

When the Assessors returned in June and July 1997 they reviewed additional written evidence and interviewed a further 133 staff. This time Assessors focused on the areas where there had been gaps during the first series of interviews. After the second round of interviews a positive report was put to a Recognition Panel on 20 August 1997. The panel decided that The Scottish Office should be recognized as an Investor in People. In total, 478 staff had been interviewed as part of the assessment process.

## BENEFITS OF INVESTORS IN PEOPLE

Working towards and achieving Investors in People status has brought about a number of benefits:

- All members of staff now have a Personal Development Plan that is reviewed at least twice a year with their manager.
- There is a greatly improved Induction system with Induction packs for all staff, including casual staff.
- A high-level Training and Development Steering Group has been set up to advise the Head of Training and Development, show top management commitment and to help evaluate training and development at organizational level.
- Evaluation of Training and Development has improved at all levels.
- A series of guidance notes for staff and managers on a range of Training and Development issues has been produced.
- Most importantly – communication has improved, with more managers now taking the time to discuss development issues with staff at least twice a year.

In a message to all staff announcing the successful outcome of the assessment, Sir Russell Hillhouse, then Permanent Secretary, referred to their achievement of Investors in People status as 'an important milestone'. There is a recognition at the most senior levels in the organization that The Scottish Office must continue to improve their training and development systems and processes and continue to encourage all staff to develop their full potential, if they are to meet the considerable challenges that face Scotland and The Scottish Office in the future.

In 1998/99 The Scottish Office underwent 'mid-term assessment' or Post Recognition Review and Development[1] at the same time as they were undergoing the major change of preparing for devolution. A number of areas for improvement were identified but The Scottish Office were delighted that they continued to be recognized as an Investor in People.

---

1   Post recognition Review and Development (PRD) was an interim assessment process. This has since been succeeded by variable timescale assessment.

## CONTENTS OF THE SCOTTISH OFFICE PORTFOLIO

### (a) Introduction to The Scottish Office

This section ran to 13 sides of A4. Its purpose was to help the Assessor understand the organization and to make her aware of any organizational issues that were felt could have an impact on the assessment.

It included general information about the structure and functions of The Scottish Office and brief details of the functions and aims of each of the five main departments and Central Services.

Details on some diverse organizational issues were also included, for example:

- The Personnel Division had been restructured about a year before assessment; an explanation of why this had occurred to set the change in a training and development context was included.
- Information Technology was having a major impact on the way the business operated with a roll out of computers onto nearly every desk halfway completed.
- The Scottish Office wanted the Assessor to understand from the outset the role of the Training and Development Unit (one of the units within Personnel Division) so it was important to explain how training budgets worked and give a rough idea of how much was spent on training and development.

### (b) A description of the training and development system

This section was designed to explain to the Assessor how the training and development systems and processes fitted with the management planning process.

### (c) The organization structure

A family tree was provided and proved to be an extremely helpful document. This item most helped the Assessor to see how all parts of the department fitted together.

### (d) A breakdown of staff

A breakdown of staff numbers by grade and department was provided. These staff statistics were designed to give the Assessor an idea of the numbers and grades of staff who worked in The Scottish Office. At this stage, the main administrative grades were included, with a list of all professional and technical staff at their administrative-equivalent level. As the interview stage of the assessment progressed the Assessor was provided with much more detail on staff statistics, including casual, professional and part-time staff.

### (e) Locations
The addresses of the main Scottish Office buildings were included so that the Assessors were able to understand the geographical spread of the organization.

### (f) The matrix of evidence
The matrix of evidence that was developed at the beginning of the collection of evidence started in 1992. It was an essential tool to allow The Scottish Office to see at a glance whether or not they had sufficient evidence to match all the indicators. It also made the Assessor's job much easier when she was reviewing the evidence against the National Standard's requirements. See Figure 6.5 for the matrix and pages 147–48 for the key to the matrix.

**Please note: The Scottish Office was assessed against the original indicators; new indicators were introduced in January 1997.**

### (g) An overview
The 'Overview against Indicators' was The Scottish Office storyboard. For each indicator a narrative was provided that gave general background to support the application. Each piece of narrative mentioned, in context, the numbered pieces of evidence that were submitted against each indicator. Each item of evidence was listed at the end of each piece of narrative. The purpose of this document was to try to help the Assessor to understand training and development in The Scottish Office and to help provide an 'audit trail', or linkages through the evidence.

### (h) The portfolio
This was the portfolio of evidence, where documents that were included were lengthy, relevant items that were highlighted for quick reference by the Assessor. All these documents were contained in polypockets with numbered index tags on their sides so that the Assessor could easily find whichever document she needed from the ring binder. Also, each polypocket, was marked clearly with the indicators that The Scottish Office believed were most relevant to that piece of evidence.

| | 1 | | | | | | 2 | | | | | | | 3 | | | | | | 4 | | | | |
|---|---|---|---|---|---|---|---|---|---|---|---|---|---|---|---|---|---|---|---|---|---|---|---|---|
| | 1 | 2 | 3 | 4 | 5 | 6 | 1 | 2 | 3 | 4 | 5 | 6 | 7 | 1 | 2 | 3 | 4 | 5 | 6 | 1 | 2 | 3 | 4 | 5 |
| 1. Permanent Secretary's Public Commitment | ✓ | | | | | | | | | | | | | | | | | | | | | | | ✓ |
| 2. Permanent Secretary's Speech to SCS | ✓ | | | | | | | | | ✓ | | | | | | | | | | | | | | ✓ |
| 3. Personnel Strategy Booklet | ✓ | | | | | | | | | ✓ | | | | | | | ✓ | | | | | | | |
| 4. Remit of IiP Board | ✓ | | | | | | | | | | | | | | | | | | | | | | | |
| 5. Secretary of State's Commitment | ✓ | | | | | | | | | | | | | | | | | | | | | | | |
| 6. 1992 Staff Survey results | | ✓ | | | | | | | | | | | | ✓ | | | | | | | | | | |
| 7. 1995 Staff Survey results | | ✓ | | | | | | ✓ | ✓ | | | | | ✓ | | ✓ | ✓ | | ✓ | | | | | |
| 8. Dept. aims, visions and values | | ✓ | | | | | | | | ✓ | | | | | | | | | | | | | | |
| 9. Draft aims, visions and values | | ✓ | | | | | | | | ✓ | | | | | | | | | | | | | | |
| 10. Departmental strategy plan | | | ✓ | ✓ | | | ✓ | | | | ✓ | | | | | | | | | | | | | |
| 11. Local plan | | | ✓ | ✓ | ✓ | | ✓ | | | | | | | | | | | | | | | | | |
| 12. Staff training and development Strategy | | | ✓ | ✓ | | | ✓ | | | | | | | | ✓ | | | | ✓ | | | ✓ | | |
| 13. End year review example | | | | ✓ | ✓ | | | ✓ | | | | | | | | | ✓ | | | | ✓ | | | |
| 14. Job appraisal review example | | | | ✓ | | | | | | | | | | | | | | | | | | | | |
| 15. Guidance note/training and development strategy | | | | ✓ | | | | | | | | | | | | | | | | | | | ✓ | |
| 16. Branch plan | | | | | ✓ | | | | | | | | | | | | | | | | | | | |
| 17. Forward job description | | | | | ✓ | | | | ✓ | | | ✓ | | | | | ✓ | ✓ | | | ✓ | | | |
| 18. In year review | | | | | ✓ | | | ✓ | ✓ | | | | | | | | ✓ | ✓ | | | | | | |

**Figure 6.5** *The Scottish Office: Investors in People – matrix of evidence*

| | 1 | | | | | | 2 | | | | | | | 3 | | | | | | 4 | | | | |
|---|---|---|---|---|---|---|---|---|---|---|---|---|---|---|---|---|---|---|---|---|---|---|---|---|
| | 1 | 2 | 3 | 4 | 5 | 6 | 1 | 2 | 3 | 4 | 5 | 6 | 7 | 1 | 2 | 3 | 4 | 5 | 6 | 1 | 2 | 3 | 4 | 5 |
| 19. Personal Development Plan | | | | | ✓ | | | ✓ | ✓ | | | ✓ | | | ✓ | | ✓ | | | | ✓ | ✓ | | |
| 20. Minutes of TUS Meeting | | | | | | ✓ | | | | | | | | | | | | | | | | | | |
| 21. Minutes of TUS Meeting | | | | | | ✓ | | | | | | | | | | | | | | | | | | |
| 22. Minutes of TUS Meeting | | | | | | ✓ | | | | | | | | | | | | | | | | | | |
| 23. Training and development Steering Group paper | | | | | | ✓ | | | | | | | | | | | | | | | | ✓ | | |
| 24. Training and development Steering Group minutes | | | | | | | ✓ | | | | | | | ✓ | | | | | ✓ | ✓ | ✓ | | ✓ | ✓ |
| 25. Staff Appraisal System outline | | | | | | | | | | ✓ | | | | | | | | | | | | | | |
| 26. New ASR workbook/guidance | | | | | | | | | | | ✓ | | | | | | | | | | | | | |
| 27. Core criteria for SCS | | | | | | | | | | | ✓ | | | | | | | | | | | | | |
| 28. Notice of ASR Training | | | | | | | | | | | | ✓ | | | | | | | | | | | | |
| 29. Ratings on development of staff | | | | | | | | | | | | ✓ | | | | | | | | | | | | |
| 30. Quarterly programme | | | | | | | | | | | | ✓ | | | | ✓ | | ✓ | | | | | | |
| 31. Pre-course Questionnaires | | | | | | | | | | | | | ✓ | | | | | | ✓ | | ✓ | | | |
| 32. Contract between development advisers and line managers | | | | | | | | | | | | | ✓ | | | | | | | | | | | |
| 33. General notice | | | | | | | | | | | | | ✓ | | | | | | | | | | | |
| 34. Examples of qualifications | | | | | | | | | | | | | ✓ | | | | | | | | | | | |
| 35. Procedures for degree studies and VFE | | | | | | | | | | | | | ✓ | | | | | | | | | | | |

Figure 6.5 continued

| | 1 | | | | | | 2 | | | | | | | 3 | | | | | | 4 | | | | |
|---|---|---|---|---|---|---|---|---|---|---|---|---|---|---|---|---|---|---|---|---|---|---|---|---|
| | 1 | 2 | 3 | 4 | 5 | 6 | 1 | 2 | 3 | 4 | 5 | 6 | 7 | 1 | 2 | 3 | 4 | 5 | 6 | 1 | 2 | 3 | 4 | 5 |
| 36. Contract to provide SVQ support | | | | | | | | | | | | | ✓ | | | | | | | | | | | |
| 37. Report of Induction Review Team | | | | | | | ✓ | | | | | | | | | | | | | | | | | |
| 38. Vacancy notice | | | | | | | ✓ | | | | | | | | | | | | | | | | | |
| 39. Training Information Notice | | | | | | | | ✓ | | | | | | | | | | | | | | | | |
| 40. Office vacancy (notices) | | | | | | | | ✓ | | | | | | | | | | | | | | | | |
| 41. Course comment sheets | | | | | | | | | | | | | | | | | | | | | ✓ | | | |

**Figure 6.5** *continued*

Original evidence

**Doc no. Brief description**

1. Permanent Secretary's public commitment, 21 November 1991
2. Permanent Secretary's speech at the launch of the Senior Civil Service
3. Personnel Strategy Booklet
4. Remit of the Investors in People Project Board
5. Secretary of State's commitment to IiP – 28 August 1995 letter refers
6. Staff attitude survey 1992 – desk drop and executive sum mary
7. Tom McGlew survey report 1995
8. Departmental 'Aims, Vision and Values'
9. Draft consultation document Mission, Vision and Values of TSO
10. Departmental Management Plan
11. Local Plan
12. Staff Development and Training Strategy
13. End-year Review
14. Job appraisal review
15. Guidance note on developing a Staff Training and Development Strategy
16. Branch Plan
17. Forward Job Description
18. In-year review
19. Personal Development Plan
20. Minutes of meetings between Management and TUS
21. Minutes of meetings between Management and TUS
22. Minutes of meetings between Management and TUS
23. Training and Development Steering Group budget paper
24. The Training and Development Steering Group minutes and papers
25. Staff Appraisal System
26. Workbook and guidance for job-holders – New Appraisal System
27. Core Criteria for the Senior Civil Service
28. Training and reporting and countersigning officers – notice
29. Staff Development box markings – data query

30. Quarterly programme
31. Pre-course questionnaires
32. Contract of work between DA and line manager
33. Establishing a Per. Function in TSO advance copy of General Notice
34. Certificates in Purchase and Supply, Personnel and Accountancy
35. Training Information Notices: Degree-level and VFE procedures/support
36. Contract with training provider to pursue SVQs
37. Induction Improvement Team report 1995
38. Vacancy Notice for Induction Project Manager
39. Variety of Training Information Notices (TIN)
40. Office Vacancy Notices
41. Course Comment sheets

## ADDITIONAL EVIDENCE PROVIDED AFTER DEFERRAL

- Evidence of each of the Departmental Management Boards evaluating spend in 1996/97
- Evaluation papers for Training and Development Steering Group on four areas of corporate spend
- IT Training
- Training for the new Appraisal system
- Finance Training
- French language training
- Extract from the minutes of the meeting at which these papers were considered
- Five examples of Staff Development and Training Strategies
- Letter from the new Secretary of State showing commitment to IiP
- Special Notice – message to all staff from the new Secretary of State
- Casuals Induction Pack and Management Notice advertising it
- Review of the Pilot Induction Pack for permanent staff
- Copies of the most recent training and development News (with Quarterly programme incorporated for the first time) and the training and development Plus
- Proof copy of the new corporate training and development strategy 'training and development in the Scottish Office' looking to the year 2000 and beyond

- Guidance note for line managers on the new Induction arrangements
- Copy of the new 'Welcome Pack' (Induction) for permanent staff
- Copy of the 'Training and Development story' linking management, planning, appraisal and training and development
- Guidance note on organizing 'Away Days'
- Revised guidance note on developing a Staff Development and Training Strategy
- Copies of communications with the TUS
- Details of training and development spend in 1996/97 and Budgets and priorities for 1997/98
- Revised Personal Development Plan encouraging personal evaluation
- Pre-training and development event briefing document for manager and participant

**THE SCOTTISH OFFICE: ADDITIONAL INFORMATION**

**1. When did The Scottish Office 'sign up'?**
The commitment was made in November 1991. At that time The Scottish Office was one of only two government departments to make the commitment to work towards the National Standard. Since then all government departments have been required to follow this route and the White Paper on Development and Training in the Civil Service, published 1 July, set stretching targets for all departments to achieve Investors in People status.

**2. Key milestones in The Scottish Office's journey to recognition**
In 1992, 20 per cent of all staff in all grades and in all locations were surveyed. It was a very complicated survey because it included all sorts of other aspects of Personnel work, including welfare, promotion, appraisal, induction, recruitment, career development and so on. Analysing the survey was very complex and the results were not available until the end of 1993. The headline results were fed back to staff at the beginning of 1994. During 1993 and 1994 systems continued to be improved and replaced to match the standard.

The Scottish Office underwent a mock assessment in 1994. The Assessor's view was that the department was not yet ready for formal assessment: some things still needed improvement. Work on systems and processes continued during the early part of 1995 and in mid-1995 a second survey was carried out – this time focusing only on training and development. The results were much more positive although the survey identified three areas where further work needed to be done. These were:

- People in The Scottish Office were still having difficulty explaining the aims and objectives of The Scottish Office. They could articulate the purpose of their division and unit and even their department, but they found it much more difficult to explain what The Scottish Office as whole existed to do.
- Induction procedures needed improving. The Scottish Office was quite good at welcoming people when they moved from one division to another but not so good at welcoming people for the first time.
- Improvements were needed to the way evaluation of the investment in training and development took place.

### 3. Why did the journey take so long?
The Training and Development Unit took a 'low key' approach to Investors in People and used the standard as a benchmark to ensure that systems and processes matched good practice.

*Preparing for assessment*

### 4. How did The Scottish Office prepare?
After the Management Group agreed the proposal that each department would be assessed in turn, The Scottish Office spoke to Departmental Management Boards about what this would involve. They compiled a core portfolio of evidence for the Assessor team to review and provided additional information on corporate issues and on individual departments as required.

### 5. Were people coached before they were interviewed?
No. A series of awareness seminars was provided for senior managers so that they would understand the process they were about to go through and so they could inform their staff. A video was made to help explain about IiP and what had been achieved over the years to work towards the National Standard.

*Assessment*

### 6. What did assessment involve?
The Lead Assessor reviewed the portfolio of evidence prepared by

Training and Development Unit. A random sample of staff were then interviewed.

**7. Who selected staff for interview?**

The Lead Assessor made all selections. During the 1996 interviews, the Assessor indicated when she would be visiting a particular part of Scotland. Heads of Divisions and Units provided a list of staff who would be available on that day. The Assessor then selected the people to be seen – including casual staff. For the 1997 interviews the Assessor selected lists of staff from the Business Directory. The staff in Training and Development Unit made the arrangements for the interviews.

**8. What did the interviews involve?**

The interviews were conducted as one-to-one interviews or focus groups, which lasted between half an hour and an hour. Confidentiality was observed. Neither senior management nor the Investors in People project team were able to identify what an individual said to the Assessor.

**9. How many people were interviewed and how were they selected?**

During the period July to November 1996 the Assessors interviewed 345 members of staff. In June and July 1997 they interviewed a further 133. On both occasions, the Assessors selected who they wanted to see, taking into account grade mix, geographical location, full-time/part-time/casual mix.

**10. What grades were interviewed and what was the geographical spread?**

A very wide range of grades, administrative, professional and support grades, from junior staff to top management. The full geographical spread of The Scottish Office and its agencies (excluding The Scottish Prison Service) was covered, from the islands in the north to Ayr and the Borders in the south.

**11. What was the outcome of The Scottish Office's first assessment (July to November 1996)?**

While she found lots of examples of good practice across the Office, the Assessor's view at that time was that The Scottish Office was not ready yet. The Assessor identified a number of gaps, asked to see additional evidence and suggested that some of the systems and processes needed a bit longer to bed in. It was agreed the Assessors would return in June 1997.

**12. What were the gaps?**

- Inconsistencies in sharing vision
- Some staff with no job descriptions or PDPs
- Confusion over roles
- Lack of clarity over resources
- Induction not very effective
- Very little by way of pre-training and development discussion and post-activity evaluation

**13. Was it unusual to be deferred?**

No. The Scottish Office were assured by Investors in People Scotland that most large organizations have to undertake some further work as a result of the first assessment.

---

The following case studies look at parts of The Scottish Office and how they approached the implementation of the European Foundation for Quality Management Excellence Model.

---

### Case study 1 – Office of the Accountant in Bankruptcy

The process began in mid-1996. The Office of the Accountant in Bankruptcy (AOB) had suffered a long and frequently unsettled time where workloads were increasing and staff numbers were not. The Office environment was poor and compounded the morale issue further. It was clear to all employees and to managers that something needed to change.

There was light on the horizon and the tide was beginning to turn. The workload had stabilized, order was being brought to the staffing position, a planned market test of some of the Office functions was abandoned and plans to move the whole Office to a new building in 1997/98 were announced. Helpful as all these things were, they needed to do something specific to rebuild staff morale and a sense of unity and purpose. The Scottish Office was progressing well on their journey towards Investors in People status and this activity was beginning to impact positively on employees. But within the AOB there was a feeling that more needed to be done. Advice from the Personnel Department pointed the way to the Excellence Model as the most appropriate way forward.

## THE PROCESS

Within the AOB there are three main constituencies: case management, a supervisory arm and support services. At the outset it was recognized that involving all staff would be critical to the success of this approach. An Away Day for all AOB staff was arranged and took place in April 1997.

A self-assessment exercise was arranged with staff organized into common functions with random multi-grade groups as follows:

- two Case Management;
- two Supervisory;
- two Support Services.

Each group was facilitated by a non-participating delegate.

The standard Excellence Model self-assessment questionnaire was adapted to make the questions more directly relevant to AOB and concentrated on just six of the nine elements that the Excellence Model contains. The elements concentrated on were:

- Leadership;
- Policy and Strategies;
- People (Staff) Satisfaction;
- Customer Satisfaction;
- Processes;
- Business Results.

Note: These elements refer to the pre-1999 version of the model.

Each group was asked to consider and discuss the questions under each heading as a group but then to record their scores as individuals. The scores were collated and compared with those of the senior management team who had undergone self-assessment a few weeks earlier. There was a surprising degree of consensus between the groups and the senior management team.

The second stage of the exercise was to ask each of the groups to offer at least four suggestions for improvement. Once again, the senior managers were impressed with the commitment of the groups to the exercise and with the quality of the suggestions made.

A constant theme from all the groups was that internal communication; particularly 'horizontal' communication, was considered an area of concern. As a first step to putting that right, AOB established a communications group to enable employees at all levels to meet at regular intervals. They also set up a Departmental Steering Group comprising representatives of all Branches and grades within their Office; their aim was to develop their own agenda and collectively form an effective multi-directional communication network. A working group was also established to oversee the development of a comprehensive manual of operational instructions, another 'consensus' recommendation that resulted from the self-assessment process.

The other suggestions made by the discussion groups as a result of self-assessement have not been implemented yet, but it is intended to remit some of these either to one or more of the established discussion groups or to 'bespoke' working groups to develop and refine the suggestions made.

It is accepted that it will take time to agree and implement all the changes necessary to make the improvements required and that the self-assessment exercise will need to be repeated; however, the journey towards continuous improvement for AOB has now begun.

---

## Case study 2 – The Scottish Executive Directorate of Administrative Services Procurement and Commercial Services Division (PCSD)

### BACKGROUND

In 1996 the Management Group approved the proposals made by The Scottish Office Purchasing and Supply Strategy paper MG (98) 16, by the then Director of Procurement (DoP). One of the proposals involved PCSD working towards ISO9000 accreditation. Early in 1997 it was concluded that ISO9000 (a quality management standard designed to control the quality of the product and service that is required by the customer) did not provide the best framework to drive forward continuous improvement. Instead, it was decided that the most appropriate way forward was through a Total Quality Management (TQM) approach to improving the effectiveness and flexibility of businesses as a whole. This approach is a way of organizing and involving the whole organization to move towards continuous improvement by constantly challenging current practices and procedures to look for better ways of working. The aim was to rid people's lives of wasted effort by involving everyone in the processes of improvement. The methods and techniques used in TQM were to be applied throughout the organization in an effort to become more effective and more efficient in all that the organization did. In considering the application of the TQM philosophy it was decided that the use of the European Foundation Quality Model for Business Excellence provided the framework necessary to achieve the objective of taking the PCSD forward. To facilitate this process the post of Quality Manager was created within PCSD, in December 1996.

## THE PROCESS

PCSD's senior management team, together with the quality manager, decided that a review of *The Scottish Office Purchasing Contracting and Supply Manual* (PCSM) was a prerequisite to establish the base for quality control. The PCSM was replaced by the *Procurement Policy Manual* (PPM), which was issued to Scottish Office senior staff in July 1997. At the same time the PPM was made available to the rest of the office in electronic format. The PPM reflects best practice as defined in the White Paper 'Setting New Standards – A Strategy for Government Procurement', and was a result of team effort to develop the new procedures. The new manual incorporated customer's views, for example, recommendations by the newly formed Procurement Advisory Board (PAB) and consultation with colleagues in various parts of the Office. The PPM was endorsed by the then Permanent Secretary, and was well received throughout the Office. Colleagues and customers alike have commented on the quality of the new PPM.

The PPM was complemented by the introduction on the intranet in October 1997 of the *Procurement Instructions Manual* (PIM), essentially a 'how to do it' procedures manual aimed at purchasers. The PIM's availability on the intranet has led to less than 100 hard copies being required across the Office since its introduction, thus resulting in value for money savings, increased efficiency and ease of updating. Together the PPM and the PIM now provide a comprehensive guide for Scottish Office procurement policy, procedures and practices, via the intranet. Both manuals are constantly being revised and updates incorporated on a regular basis.

During this development period, PCSD's quality manager attended various Scottish Office Quality Network and Quality Scotland

Foundation (QSF) events. These activities allowed the PCSD to develop approaches to achieve quality improvements within PCSD. A Communication Strategy Project Team was established in 1997 to review and improve internal communication. This team was very much staff initiated and comprised of a wide cross-section of all employees. April 1998 saw the introduction of PCSD's Communication Strategy, which is designed to promote clear, efficient communication within PCSD in order to improve its effectiveness.

All staff in PCSD were involved in the first self-assessment based on the Excellence Model for Business Excellence approach to continuous improvement. The small-to-medium enterprise edition was used as this version of the model provided the best fit with the size and structure of the PCSD. The self-assessment process took place between December 1997 and February 1998. A final version of the PCSD's self-assessment report and action plans was produced and refined by PCSD staff assisted by the facilitator and then made available to all staff in PCSD via the Team Library in August 1998. The Quality Management Group now provides a quarterly Management Progress Report to the Director of Procurement (DoP). This ensures that the DoP is aware of progress being made.

## Case study 3 – The Scottish Education Department

### HM Inspectors of Schools (HMI)

A main role of HM Inspectors of Schools is to act as professional evaluators in Scottish education. A key aspect of the approach to this work is that HMI engage in a great deal of self-evaluation of their working practices. For example, HMI continually review procedures and arrangements for inspecting and reporting on educational establishments and use people and customer satisfaction questionnaires during inspections. The usual range of communication links and business meetings as well as annual reporting provide feedback on the functioning of the organization and allow HMI to take action for continuous improvement. However, it was recognized that there were gaps in the self-assessment process and that some of the evaluation questionnaires were becoming ritualistic with diminishing returns in terms of useful management information.

Through HMI's work with schools and education authorities, they were introduced to Quality Scotland Foundation (QSF) and the European Foundation for Quality Management Excellence Model in the context of a project, linking the Excellence Model to school self-evaluation. HMI and schools employ a common set of performance indicators for external and internal evaluation.

To investigate whether this approach could be used to improve the assessment of schools and educational establishments, an HMI undertook the Excellence Model assessor training and from this training was able to demonstrate the strong links between the Excellence Model and the approaches already established in schools for self-assessment. It was clear that there were many common principles. It was later that the potential of the Excellence Model for HMI's own business was explored.

Having recognized the need to adopt a structured approach to self-evaluation, HMI arranged, with the help of Andy McAlpine from The Scottish Office Training and Development Unit, a Facilitated Assessment for Chief Executives (FACE) session during which the HMI management group engaged in self-assessment. From this initial session a series of priorities for action were identified. Many of the areas for action had already been identified and this gave confidence to those involved that the Excellence Model approach was robust and would provide a framework for further evaluation.

A significant gap that had already been noted was scarcity of staff at certain grades in the overall complement of people across Scotland and the subsequent difficulties in harmonizing staff development and ensuring effective communication. The self-assessment process enabled a review of the staffing structures and functions to take place. This resulted in freeing up professional HMIs to be more highly geared in their work activity, creating greater value for money and improved efficiencies.

HMI approached the use of the Excellence Model approach with a critical eye and started to develop a number of other avenues in parallel, all complementary. They set up a small team to coordinate developments, which included senior management, HMIs and administrative staff. The task of this group was to consider 'How good is our Inspectorate?'. Next, the language of Facilitated Assessment for Chief Executives training session and EFQM criteria was customized to be directly relevant to the Inspectorate's work. As part of this process HMI mapped the functions of the Inspectorate across the nine elements of the Excellence Model and defined the key processes that they used. Space in the programme for an extended session at an HMI national conference provided feedback and ideas on taking the systematic self-evaluation of the organization forward.

The ideas generated from the conference were mapped on to the Excellence Model structure to identify gaps and self-analytical tools and sources of information which were already part of the system and which could be exploited for self-evaluation. HMI's view is, 'if it's there, use it and don't waste time developing new structures and tools'.

A professional agency was employed to consult with a range of focus groups representing those associated with schools (senior managers, teachers, parents) to provide 'customer' feedback. This was complemented on an annual basis by HMI using internal customers within the organization and more widely in other Scottish Executive policy divisions.

In line with the HMI's professional work in schools and their interactions with the Accounts Commission and Best Value developments, the various strands are being brought together into a coherent approach to continuous review in a cyclical and systematic way. HMI will in future be in a strong position to answer their self-imposed question: 'How good is our Inspectorate?'

---

**Case study 4 – The Scottish Office: Solicitor's Office**

## INTRODUCTION

The Scottish Office Solicitor's Office first looked seriously at quality issues in mid-1996 when they were working on the implementation of the Ramsay Report: a report on the future shape and structure of the Solicitor's Office. In June 1996 the Solicitor's Office was preparing a tender in a market test situation and that exercise clearly indicated to the team that there were areas for improvement in their working practices. It was decided that quality and proof of the Office's ability to deliver were areas of the business that had to be addressed in a more systematic manner.

In the light of the Office's experiences with the market test exercise and in the context of some limited involvement with The Scottish Office Quality Network, assistance was sought from The Scottish Office Training and Development Unit. In September 1996 the Deputy Solicitor and Office Practice Manager attended an awareness workshop arranged by the Training and Development Unit to explore the use of self-assessment against the Excellence Model for Business Excellence.

It was recognized immediately that the approach underlying self-assessment was unlike anything the Solicitor's Office had undertaken previously. However, they found that the questionnaire used was clear and comprehensive and, if completed honestly, would provide a valuable assessment of the efficiency and effectiveness of an organization. The fact that the questionnaire was not oriented to the Solicitor's Office was not a problem in that it was clear from initial contact with this approach that the technique was flexible and could be applied to any area of Scottish Office activity.

## MANAGEMENT BOARD CONFERENCE

Following on from the initial self-assessment and having considered recommendations from the Deputy Solicitor and the Practice Manager, the Solicitor's Office Management Board held its first conference during the weekend 29/30 November 1996. The principal purpose of the conference was to consider quality issues. High on the agenda of the conference was the completion of the self-assessment questionnaire.

At a follow-up session the results of the questionnaire were analysed. The analysis of the questionnaire results allowed consideration of the scores against the Office's critical success factors. This comparison of results revealed a number of areas for improvement under the headings of:

- customers and clients;
- people management/people satisfaction;
- processes and procedures.

Each of the areas detailed above was followed up systematically in the weeks following the conference. Pairs of senior managers were asked to consider each topic further, in consultation with clients and other senior managers as appropriate, and report back to the

Management Board. Progress has been made in all the areas mentioned, for example:

- The Office now has in place clearly defined aims and objectives.
- A communications strategy has been drafted.
- In-house training has been introduced through monthly seminars to assist staff to achieve Law Society mandatory training targets.
- Staff morale issues are being addressed in a systematic manner.

Most of the initial activity that took place was focused on the internal arrangements within the Solicitor's Office. It was recognized early in pursuit of business excellence that the Office had to address the whole business and that by addressing internal issues first, this would assist in delivering quality services to clients.

The Solicitor's Office did not approach the issues raised through applying the Excellence Model approach on the basis that items for action can be ticked off on a checklist. Rather the approach taken was more holistic in recognition that a number of ingredients are needed if business excellence is to be achieved. The Office started by looking at and addressing those issues that affected the internal functioning of the business and began devising a quality system that was client focused. The Management Board therefore agreed to follow up the conference with a workshop, which was arranged for September 1997. The focus of the workshop was client care and aimed to reassess whether the efforts of the past year had been successful. Members of the Board completed the self-assessment questionnaire for a second time and the results were analysed and compared with those results previously taken in the first exercise. This comparison was made in advance of the workshop to facilitate discussion on areas that had improved and to highlight where further action needed to be taken. A cross-section of clients were surveyed using questionnaires to ensure results were robust. An employee survey was also undertaken to measure the perceptions of employees with regard to the improvements made.

## CONCLUSIONS

The Solicitor's Office has found that the Excellence Model approach to self-assessment and continuous improvement proved to be extremely valuable in identifying and prioritizing areas for improvement and in measuring progress in achieving these improvements. A key lesson was the use of a well-trained facilitator to ensure that the approach is optimized.

Note: The scores for each of the case studies used have not been shown. It was not felt that this information would have added sufficient value to the text and was therefore not included.

## Summary

**Benchmarking**

The European Foundation for Quality Management Excellence Model is a wide-ranging organizational development tool that can be applied to any working environment. It can assist with benchmarking the performance of parts of an organization against other parts. It is able to provide the basis through which organizations can benchmark their approaches to business development against others within their industry or indeed outside their industry where processes can be identified that will provide continuous improvement opportunities. The model should be viewed as bigger than simply an award; it is an umbrella model that can provide a solid framework to integrate a number of approaches to quality improvement. Above all, it is a tool that when applied over time will provide clarity of action for any organization that wishes to improve its position in the marketplace: this is true of all organizations, whether they operate in the private or the public sector.

## Exercise 6.1

1. Using the questionnaire provided (Figure 6.6), answer each of the questions in order and use the summary at the end of each section to collate your responses.
2. Use the action plan to note the areas for development you have noted.
3. Take your collated responses and transfer these to the grid shown in Figure 6.7.
4. Use the grid shown in Figure 6.7 to note your score. From here you can now work out the points you have allocated for each element across the whole model.

For each question, tick the box that is closest to where you believe best reflects your organization's current position. Do not spend too much time completing the questionnaire and remember that it is the organization and not your personal approach that you are measuring.

## Scoring

5: This action is a natural part of the way the whole organization works.

4: I have seen this happen in some parts of the organization and it is part of a planned process.

3: I have seen this happen in some parts of the organization, but it is not reviewed and improved.

2: This happens occasionally, but it is isolated and unplanned.

1: I have heard about this idea and its intentions, but have never seen any action.

0: I have not seen or heard of any plans to do this in the organization.

After you have completed the questionnaire, transfer your results to the grid at the end of this section. Use the grid to calculate your organization's score.

Repeat the process at least once every year.

Use the scoring grid to transfer your scores for each part of the model. Calculate the points out of 1,000 using the grid.

# Leadership

**How leaders develop and facilitate the achievement of the mission and vision, develop values required for long-term success and implement these via appropriate actions and behaviours, and are personally involved in ensuring that the organization's management system is developed and implemented.**

**Scoring**

5:  This action is a natural part of the way the whole organization works.
4:  I have seen this happen in some parts of the organization and it is part of a planned process.
3:  I have seen this happen in some parts of the organization, but it is not reviewed and improved.
2:  This happens occasionally, but it is isolated and unplanned.
1:  I have heard about this idea and its intentions, but have never seen any action.
0:  I have not seen or heard of any plans to do this in the organization.

| Are Managers: | 5 | 4 | 3 | 2 | 1 | 0 | Sub Total |
|---|---|---|---|---|---|---|---|
| 1. Highly visible and regularly talk to employees. | ☐ | ☐ | ☐ | ☐ | ☐ | ☐ | ☐ |
| 2. Inspire quality through their activities and behaviour. | ☐ | ☐ | ☐ | ☐ | ☐ | ☐ | ☐ |
| 3. Act as role models in leading and supporting the realization of the organization's goals, values and corporate objectives. | ☐ | ☐ | ☐ | ☐ | ☐ | ☐ | ☐ |
| 4. Review and improve the effectiveness of their own leadership style. | ☐ | ☐ | ☐ | ☐ | ☐ | ☐ | ☐ |
| 5. Encourage employees to be innovative and promote an environment where employees are Allowed, Willing and Able[1]. | ☐ | ☐ | ☐ | ☐ | ☐ | ☐ | ☐ |
| 6. Support employees and provide appropriate backup and support. | ☐ | ☐ | ☐ | ☐ | ☐ | ☐ | ☐ |
| 7. Communicate to employees what the organization expects of them and provide feedback on what is happening. | ☐ | ☐ | ☐ | ☐ | ☐ | ☐ | ☐ |
| 8. Ensure that employees understand the implications of quality management. | ☐ | ☐ | ☐ | ☐ | ☐ | ☐ | ☐ |
| 9. Make sure that products and services design and delivery involve customers and suppliers. | ☐ | ☐ | ☐ | ☐ | ☐ | ☐ | ☐ |
| **Total points** | | | | | | | ☐ |

[1]Borzony P, Dadge R, and Hunter K (1997) *Practical Magic*, P Honey Publications, ISBN 0-9524389-4-1

Human. L (1991) *Educating Managers in a Changing South Africa*, Juta

**Figure 6.6** *EFQM self-assessment questionnaire*

## People

How the organization manages, develops and releases the knowledge and full potential of its people at an individual, team-based and organization-wide level, and plan these activities in order to support its policy and strategy and the effective operation of its processes.

### Scoring

5: This action is a natural part of the way the whole organization works.
4: I have seen this happen in some parts of the organization and it is part of a planned process.
3: I have seen this happen in some parts of the organization, but it is not reviewed and improved.
2: This happens occasionally, but it is isolated and unplanned.
1: I have heard about this idea and its intentions, but have never seen any action.
0: I have not seen or heard of any plans to do this in the organization.

| Does the organization: | 5 | 4 | 3 | 2 | 1 | 0 | Sub Total |
|---|---|---|---|---|---|---|---|
| 1. Pursue an employee development and training programme that involves the whole workforce. | ☐ | ☐ | ☐ | ☐ | ☐ | ☐ | ☐ |
| 2. Develop the skills, knowledge, attitudes and competencies to meet the organization's strategic goals. | ☐ | ☐ | ☐ | ☐ | ☐ | ☐ | ☐ |
| 3. Build teams at all levels and with other departments. | ☐ | ☐ | ☐ | ☐ | ☐ | ☐ | ☐ |
| 4. Support and encourage employees to achieve individual goals and to have pride in the job. | ☐ | ☐ | ☐ | ☐ | ☐ | ☐ | ☐ |
| 5. Allow employees to take responsibility and ownership for their own work. | ☐ | ☐ | ☐ | ☐ | ☐ | ☐ | ☐ |
| 6. Encourage employees to find innovative solutions to problem areas and act on their suggestions. | ☐ | ☐ | ☐ | ☐ | ☐ | ☐ | ☐ |
| 7. Commit to employee development and satisfaction through the promotion of organizational values and recognition schemes. | ☐ | ☐ | ☐ | ☐ | ☐ | ☐ | ☐ |
| 8. Ensure that people issues such as conditions of service and employee development are addressed. | ☐ | ☐ | ☐ | ☐ | ☐ | ☐ | ☐ |
| **Total points** | | | | | | | ☐ |

**Figure 6.6** *continued*

## Policy and Strategy

**How the organization implements its mission and vision via a clear stakeholder-focused strategy, supported by relevant policies, plans, objectives, targets and processes.**

### Scoring

5: This action is a natural part of the way the whole organization works.
4: I have seen this happen in some parts of the organization and it is part of a planned process.
3: I have seen this happen in some parts of the organization, but it is not reviewed and improved.
2: This happens occasionally, but it is isolated and unplanned.
1: I have heard about this idea and its intentions, but have never seen any action.
0: I have not seen or heard of any plans to do this in the organization.

| Does the organization: | 5 | 4 | 3 | 2 | 1 | 0 | Sub Total |
|---|---|---|---|---|---|---|---|
| 1. Use the organization's goals and values as the primary drivers for its activities. | ❑ | ❑ | ❑ | ❑ | ❑ | ❑ | ❑ |
| 2. Ensure activities support corporate strategy and policies. | ❑ | ❑ | ❑ | ❑ | ❑ | ❑ | ❑ |
| 3. Understand the political, economic, and social technological factors that affect us. | ❑ | ❑ | ❑ | ❑ | ❑ | ❑ | ❑ |
| 4. Challenge the status quo if activities do not meet corporate objectives. | ❑ | ❑ | ❑ | ❑ | ❑ | ❑ | ❑ |
| 5. Promote and manage change. | ❑ | ❑ | ❑ | ❑ | ❑ | ❑ | ❑ |
| 6. Review organizational function, design and delivery methods. | ❑ | ❑ | ❑ | ❑ | ❑ | ❑ | ❑ |
| 7. Identify how stakeholders can add value in the organization's activities. | ❑ | ❑ | ❑ | ❑ | ❑ | ❑ | ❑ |
| **Total points** | | | | | | | ❑ |

**Figure 6.6** *continued*

## Partnership and Resources

**How the organization plans and manages its external partnerships and internal resources in order to support its policy and strategy and effective operation of its processes.**

### Scoring

5: This action is a natural part of the way the whole organization works.
4: I have seen this happen in some parts of the organization and it is part of a planned process.
3: I have seen this happen in some parts of the organization, but it is not reviewed and improved.
2: This happens occasionally, but it is isolated and unplanned.
1: I have heard about this idea and its intentions, but have never seen any action.
0: I have not seen or heard of any plans to do this in the organization.

| Does the organization: | 5 | 4 | 3 | 2 | 1 | 0 | Sub Total |
|---|---|---|---|---|---|---|---|
| 1. Align resource allocation to the organization's goals and values. | ❏ | ❏ | ❏ | ❏ | ❏ | ❏ | ❏ |
| 2. Have the necessary expertise to manage resources. | ❏ | ❏ | ❏ | ❏ | ❏ | ❏ | ❏ |
| 3. Have appropriate financial system that will provide accurate and timely information. | ❏ | ❏ | ❏ | ❏ | ❏ | ❏ | ❏ |
| 4. Provide good communication channels throughout the organization and with partner organizations. | ❏ | ❏ | ❏ | ❏ | ❏ | ❏ | ❏ |
| 5. Realise the potential of new technology. | ❏ | ❏ | ❏ | ❏ | ❏ | ❏ | ❏ |
| 6. Provide appropriate resources that help employees and partners to achieve their goals. | ❏ | ❏ | ❏ | ❏ | ❏ | ❏ | ❏ |
| 7. Have well-defined procedures that ensure quality products and service delivery. | ❏ | ❏ | ❏ | ❏ | ❏ | ❏ | ❏ |
| **Total points** | | | | | | | ❏ |

**Figure 6.6** *continued*

# Processes

**How the organization designs, manages and improves its processes in order to support its policy and strategy and fully satisfy, and generate increasing value for, its customers and other stakeholders.**

### Scoring

5: This action is a natural part of the way the whole organization works.
4: I have seen this happen in some parts of the organization and it is part of a planned process.
3: I have seen this happen in some parts of the organization, but it is not reviewed and improved.
2: This happens occasionally, but it is isolated and unplanned.
1: I have heard about this idea and its intentions, but have never seen any action.
0: I have not seen or heard of any plans to do this in the organization.

| Does the organization: | 5 | 4 | 3 | 2 | 1 | 0 | Sub Total |
|---|---|---|---|---|---|---|---|
| 1. Identify key processes that support the success of the organization. | ☐ | ☐ | ☐ | ☐ | ☐ | ☐ | ☐ |
| 2. Identify ownership of key processes within the organization. | ☐ | ☐ | ☐ | ☐ | ☐ | ☐ | ☐ |
| 3. Establish standards for key processes and monitor the application of these standards. | ☐ | ☐ | ☐ | ☐ | ☐ | ☐ | ☐ |
| 4. Ensure that key processes used do not conflict with those used by suppliers. | ☐ | ☐ | ☐ | ☐ | ☐ | ☐ | ☐ |
| 5. Implement evaluation mechanisms to ensure key processes contribute to the success of the organization. | ☐ | ☐ | ☐ | ☐ | ☐ | ☐ | ☐ |
| 6. Encourage the innovation and creativity of employees to improve key processes. | ☐ | ☐ | ☐ | ☐ | ☐ | ☐ | ☐ |
| 7. Use feedback from customers and suppliers to generate creative and innovative solutions to process management issues. | ☐ | ☐ | ☐ | ☐ | ☐ | ☐ | ☐ |
| **Total points** | | | | | | | ☐ |

**Figure 6.6** *continued*

## Customer Results

**What the organization is achieving in relation to the satisfaction of its external customers.**

### Scoring

5: This action is a natural part of the way the whole organization works.
4: I have seen this happen in some parts of the organization and it is part of a planned process.
3: I have seen this happen in some parts of the organization, but it is not reviewed and improved.
2: This happens occasionally, but it is isolated and unplanned.
1: I have heard about this idea and its intentions, but have never seen any action.
0: I have not seen or heard of any plans to do this in the organization.

**Does the organization:**      **5 4 3 2 1 0 Sub Total**

1. Have an established system to identify:

   • Customers' perceptions    ❑ ❑ ❑ ❑ ❑ ❑ ❑

   • Indicators of customer satisfaction    ❑ ❑ ❑ ❑ ❑ ❑ ❑

   • Customer development needs and expectations    ❑ ❑ ❑ ❑ ❑ ❑ ❑

   • Customers' confidence    ❑ ❑ ❑ ❑ ❑ ❑ ❑

2. Involve employees in action plans to address customers' issues.    ❑ ❑ ❑ ❑ ❑ ❑ ❑

3. Compare itself through benchmarking, to other organizations.    ❑ ❑ ❑ ❑ ❑ ❑ ❑

               **Total points**    ❑

**Figure 6.6** *continued*

# People Results

**What the organization is achieving in relation to its people.**

## Scoring

5: This action is a natural part of the way the whole organization works.

4: I have seen this happen in some parts of the organization and it is part of a planned process.

3: I have seen this happen in some parts of the organization, but it is not reviewed and improved.

2: This happens occasionally, but it is isolated and unplanned.

1: I have heard about this idea and its intentions, but have never seen any action.

0: I have not seen or heard of any plans to do this in the organization.

| Does the organization: | 5 | 4 | 3 | 2 | 1 | 0 | Sub Total |
|---|---|---|---|---|---|---|---|
| 1. Identify key indicators of people satisfaction. | ☐ | ☐ | ☐ | ☐ | ☐ | ☐ | ☐ |
| 2. Measure employees' satisfaction through surveys, direct interviews and other methods. | ☐ | ☐ | ☐ | ☐ | ☐ | ☐ | ☐ |
| 3. Understand and act on employees' concerns. | ☐ | ☐ | ☐ | ☐ | ☐ | ☐ | ☐ |
| 4. Identify and act on constantly repeating issues. | ☐ | ☐ | ☐ | ☐ | ☐ | ☐ | ☐ |
| 5. Involve itself in benchmarking activities. | ☐ | ☐ | ☐ | ☐ | ☐ | ☐ | ☐ |
| **Total points** | | | | | | | ☐ |

**Figure 6.6** *continued*

## Society Results

**What the organization is achieving in relation to local, national and international society as appropriate.**

### Scoring

5: This action is a natural part of the way the whole organization works.
4: I have seen this happen in some parts of the organization and it is part of a planned process.
3: I have seen this happen in some parts of the organization, but it is not reviewed and improved.
2: This happens occasionally, but it is isolated and unplanned.
1: I have heard about this idea and its intentions, but have never seen any action.
0: I have not seen or heard of any plans to do this in the organization.

| Does the organization: | 5 | 4 | 3 | 2 | 1 | 0 | Sub Total |
|---|---|---|---|---|---|---|---|
| 1. Consider the impact of its actions on the community where it operates. | ❏ | ❏ | ❏ | ❏ | ❏ | ❏ | ❏ |
| 2. Provide information on its actions to the community where it operates. | ❏ | ❏ | ❏ | ❏ | ❏ | ❏ | ❏ |
| 3. Act as a responsible citizen. | ❏ | ❏ | ❏ | ❏ | ❏ | ❏ | ❏ |
| 4. Provide medical, social and leisure facilities for the community where it operates. | ❏ | ❏ | ❏ | ❏ | ❏ | ❏ | ❏ |
| 5. Ensure noise and other nuisances are minimized through adequate measures. | ❏ | ❏ | ❏ | ❏ | ❏ | ❏ | ❏ |
| **Total points** | | | | | | | ❏ |

**Figure 6.6** *continued*

# Key Performance Results

**What the organization is achieving in relation to its planned performance.**

**Scoring**

5: This action is a natural part of the way the whole organization works.
4: I have seen this happen in some parts of the organization and it is part of a planned process.
3: I have seen this happen in some parts of the organization, but it is not reviewed and improved.
2: This happens occasionally, but it is isolated and unplanned.
1: I have heard about this idea and its intentions, but have never seen any action.
0: I have not seen or heard of any plans to do this in the organization.

| Does the organization: | 5 | 4 | 3 | 2 | 1 | 0 | Sub Total |
|---|---|---|---|---|---|---|---|
| 1. Have a clear statement of performance indicators that reflect its goals and targets. | ☐ | ☐ | ☐ | ☐ | ☐ | ☐ | ☐ |
| 2. Improve trends in key results areas. | ☐ | ☐ | ☐ | ☐ | ☐ | ☐ | ☐ |
| 3. Use review processes to inform Strategic Action Plans. | ☐ | ☐ | ☐ | ☐ | ☐ | ☐ | ☐ |
| 4. Establish and measure key result areas that will improve organizational performance. | ☐ | ☐ | ☐ | ☐ | ☐ | ☐ | ☐ |
| 5. Benchmark its results against sectoral, national and global trends. | ☐ | ☐ | ☐ | ☐ | ☐ | ☐ | ☐ |
| **Total points** | | | | | | | ☐ |

**Figure 6.6** *continued*

Use the scoring grid to transfer your scores for each part of the model. Calculate the points out of 1,000 using the grid.

The EFQM model score is calculated from a possible total of 1000 points. To convert your score from the questionnaire, multiply each score by 3.57 before entering it into the grid. Then use the factor to multiply your score to see the total points out of 1000.

Scoring grid

| Criterion | Score awarded | Factor | Points awarded |
|---|---|---|---|
| 1. Leadership | | x 1.0 | |
| 2. Policy and Strategy | | x 0.8 | |
| 3. People | | x 0.9 | |
| 4. Partnerships and Resources | | x 0.9 | |
| 5. Processes | | x 1.4 | |
| 6. Customer Results | | x 2.0 | |
| 7. People Results | | x 0.9 | |
| 8. Society Results | | x 0.6 | |
| 9. Key Performance Results | | x 1.5 | |
| Total Points Awards | //////////////////////////////////////////////////// | ///////////////////////////////////// | |

**Figure 6.7** *Self-assessment scoring grid*

# ◄ CHAPTER 7 ►

# THE CHANGING FACE OF WORK

*Everything flows and nothing remains unchanged.*

Ancient Greek philosopher

## Some recent trends in the workplace

**Empowering employees**

There are a number of key changes in the economy that are driving changes in the way that we work. One of the main drivers of change has been the move from scientific management principles as described by Taylor, which were promoted and popularized by Ford. A fundamental shift in the organization of companies has begun to emerge from these principles, with a shift towards empowering employees through greater participation in the workplace. The reasons for this change are multiple:

- globalization of the economy and the competitive environment where exposure to best practice forces standards to rise;
- market maturity with increasingly sophisticated customers that demand continuously improved products and services;
- barriers to entry in markets increasingly being removed;

- augmented products and services becoming the norm – products and services alone are no longer sufficient to satisfy the demands of the customer base;
- growth in the service sector as an important market bringing increased demands on providers to differentiate their products and services from others.

These changes have brought with them a need to move away from basing competitiveness on hard factors such as physical or financial resources, economies of scale or product design towards softer factors such as core competencies, reputation, speed to market and level of service. A whole new approach to business is emerging as we enter the 21st century.

**A new approach to business**

The organization of the workplace and the attitudes to work are fundamental factors in the success for this new environment. For organizations to survive or indeed to thrive in this environment requires a rethink of the way in which work is organized and products or services delivered. Thrival[1] in the future will depend on organizations' ability to face these challenges and adapt quickly to the changes they face. There is no one single approach that will ensure thrival; however, there are basic approaches already being adopted in the best organizations that will help. The companies featured in this book exhibit many of the following features:

**Thrival**

- a cultural shift towards greater participation, team working, devolved responsibilities, process-based approaches to work and market-focused delivery;
- increased investment in education, training and development of core competencies that will improve job skills, increase learning and create more flexible approaches to work;
- flatter organizational structures with increasing use of outsourcing, and partnership working with suppliers and customers with an emphasis on quality improvement techniques such as continuous improvement;
- matrix management systems to organize flexible teams capable of responding to customer demands more quickly with a corresponding increase in flexible working patterns, working hours, multi-skilled employees;

---

1 Tom Boydell, Organizational Consultant

- use of performance measurement and management systems that reward the whole organization in financial terms but that also benefit employees through better rewards;
- reward systems that focus on the new methods of working through rewards for increased knowledge, profit sharing and share ownership all designed to improve individual and organizational excellence.

All of the factors above reflect that the workplace is changing, that customers are more sophisticated and that employees require to be managed in a more dynamic way than in the past. We are living in the knowledge economy and need to accept that this quiet revolution has taken a strong grip of the environment in which we live and work.

**The knowledge economy**

The knowledge economy has placed a new challenge before us. In response the workplace is changing to adapt to meet these demands. It is clear that many organizations are already changing – but how? The range of approaches is vast, but commonly organizations are moving towards integrated systems of managing their businesses. Many are adopting key processes as their business focus, moving away from functional or product-based structures. This move allows the company to capitalize on the knowledge that employees have of the market and how the business operates. By creating a key process approach to product or service delivery, companies can respond more quickly to changing demands.

**Key processes**

Focusing on key processes within the business can also bring other changes such as a reduction in the number of functional-specific teams. By integrating processes, many organizations find that dedicated teams are no longer an efficient or effective way to operate. In many instances this means that teams previously considered specialist now form part of a core team which focuses on customer needs. Designers, marketing specialists and finance support can now be found to work in multi-disciplined teams based on a market-led business need.

**Self-managed teams**

With these changes, the need for several management layers is frequently removed. Self-managed teams are capable of negotiating direct with customers and suppliers to respond to their needs more quickly. Organizing purchases and supplying goods become more efficient if the supply chain is short. For this process to operate efficiently, teams must act in a semi-autonomous manner and so management structures need to reflect this change.

Continuous improvement processes are becoming the norm within the workplace. Quality management systems such as Investors in

People, EFQM, BS EN ISO 9000 and many others are all being applied within the workplace to improve working methods and to provide structures through which companies can gain competitive advantage.

In recognition that people are the deliverers of the products and services that companies produce, there has been a shift towards improved training and development for employees. Increased investment in this area is now viewed by progressive organizations not as a luxury or as a reward for good behaviour but as a key business process that leads to market success.

Alongside this increase in training and development has been a growth in effective reward systems that provide a mechanism through which employees can engage with the organization in ways never before considered usual. Profit sharing in many forms is part of the empowering agenda that is sweeping through organizations that recognize that the knowledge and skills of their employees are the key differential that makes them successful in the marketplace.

**Employees are the key differential to business success**

## Facing up to the challenge of change

Change is the one constant we can rely on. There are similarities in the phases of organizational and personal change. Figure 7.1 shows a typical reaction to change. It is possible to relate this 'coping cycle' to the whole organization experiencing change in working conditions or practices. First, there is denial or resistance where defence of the old methods of working is foremost with questions of 'why change?' and scepticism of the need for change dominating the debate. Next, old practices or habits are discarded in favour of new ones and new systems are adopted. Eventually the new practices are viewed as the norm and the cycle begins again as yet more changes are introduced.

**The coping cycle**

1. Denial 2. Defence 3. Discarding 4. Adoption 5. Internalization

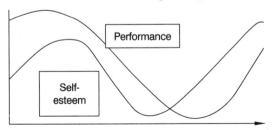

**Figure 7.1** *The coping cycle*

**From denial to internalization**

The time associated with each stage of the cycle varies, depending upon circumstances. It may be that in large organizations a particular department or group may adapt more quickly. However the change cycle is applied, it is essential that people and organizations move quickly from denial to internalization of new approaches more and more quickly. Change is the fundamental process through which we learn, develop and in business grow. It is clear from the figure that performance and self-esteem are closely related. People need to feel good about themselves to be able to perform well. Change introduces uncertainty and can create pressure for individuals and whole organizations that in turn affects performance. Confidence and self-worth are essential if performance is to improve. It is for this reason that change has to be managed effectively; if not, the drop in performance associated with changing processes might not recover quickly enough for the change to have merited implementation.

Changing the way we work, becoming more flexible, adapting quickly and accepting the need to buy-in to new ideas and approaches are all essential competencies of the modern worker. Technical skills can be taught, but attitudes must be nurtured and learnt. The new knowledge economy demands a workforce that is skilled, motivated and able to accept change.

## Whose job is it anyway?

There are always winners and losers in all aspects of life. Organizations that are adapting now will be the winners of the future and people who accept that they need to improve their knowledge and skills continuously will join this band of achievers. We all have a personal responsibility to move with the times or be left behind. It is essential then that access to opportunity is open to everyone and that we all play our individual part in the knowledge economy.

We live in a society that is not always fair or even-handed in the way that opportunity is created or accessed. Social factors often impact hardest where the need is greatest. Employers and governments have a part to play in redistributing wealth and in creating opportunity but individuals must also take responsibility if they are to make the most of these chances. Good employers recognize that the potential of their employees can be enhanced through education, training and development and many are forming partnerships with their employees and local education providers to improve the life skills of their workforce.

**Forming partnerships**

For individuals it is essential that the barriers to participation within the workplace are removed and that the idea of learning while at work is viewed as a normal business activity. For employers this means finding ways of making such developments attractive and relevant to their business needs. The National Standard Investors in People provides a framework to structure learning and development into normal business practices while achieving improved business results. Employability for the future will depend on a continuous cycle of improving knowledge, skills and developing an adaptable attitude towards change. With the help of forward-thinking organizations and supportive government policies we can all embrace the culture of thrival.

**Employability**

## A flexible me

Consider for a moment the changes that have taken place in your own working life. How many changes of job have you had in the past five years? How many new systems or approaches have you adopted as part of the changes around you? Outside work, what changes have you faced and how did you cope with them? Some changes have created no opportunity to resist; there will have been circumstances beyond your personal control that have meant you needed to accept that you would never be the same again. Often in work we find it easier to complain or resist change because we can depersonalize what is happening. We can blame the company for forcing us to change, we can point to other companies that are better to work for and we can normally find a reason why the company we work for is not as good as it could be. And yet we are resistant to changes because we view them as inconvenient, tiresome or challenging our comfort-zone. Getting uncomfortable might be the key to success, yet we still refuse to buy-in to new ideals or approaches. Our attitude to change is crucial to our personal success and to the success of the organizations we work for. So what's the recipe for success, how do we become comfortable with the uncomfortable? Table 7.1 looks at some of the barriers to change and how to overcome them.

**Challenging our comfort-zone**

**Table 7.1** *Barriers to change and how to overcome them*

| Barriers | Methods to overcome barriers |
| --- | --- |
| Unawareness or lack of information | Education and improved communications, establish self-interest in change. |
| Lack of priority – change programmes | Establish change as a normal pattern of work. |

**Table 7.1** *continued*

| Barriers | Methods to overcome barriers |
|---|---|
| May not be given priority and impact is lost in day-to-day business activity. | Provide training and education. For change, establish targets and measures of success, review procedures and reward systems, involve all levels of management and staff. |
| Sub-optimization of resources or lack of commitment. | Increase participation levels – get involved! Work across teams and use diagonal slices of the organization to implement and monitor change. |
| Cultural patterns and myths – failures of the past can affect future programmes. | Check out the culture – what kind of environment are we working in? Undertake surveys and find out the real barriers to change and how to deal with resistance. |

Table 7.1 is not meant to be exhaustive and much of what it represents can be applied at individual and corporate levels. The key message is simple. Each of us has a responsibility to be as flexible as possible and we need to be mature enough to recognize that there are times when we will resist change, but we also need to look for ways to overcome our personal resistance if we are to thrive.

## Continuing to improve

The National Standard Investors in People and the Excellence Model are tools for improving organizational effectiveness and efficiency. Both models have undergone recent changes to ensure that they remain current and relevant to the world of work. Both are likely to continue to change over time to maintain their relevance and to improve the ability of organizations to strive for ever-better performance. Recently the Excellence Model introduced the ideas of working in partnership and knowledge management, and strengthened that part of the model that deals with the management of people. These changes and others were made in recognition of the changing emphasis in organizations on how we work and on the trends identified by users of the model.

**Knowledge management**

Investors in People has also changed and current developments are considering how the model links to the concept of the learning organization and levels of learning. These changes will be introduced at an appropriate time and will add to the Standard's ability to grow flexibly with changes in our society. Fundamentally the concept of integrating people planning into the strategic planning function of an organization will remain at the heart of the National Standard. With the increasing need for continuous improvement in all aspects of our lives it is refreshing to know that models such as Investors in People and the Excellence Model can adapt over time, without diminishing the integrity of the approaches both promote.

## What if?

As the National Standard continues to develop to meet and drive market changes, innovation in organizational approaches begin to emerge. Trends in development over time reflect the growth in intellectual capability and organizations need to move with these changes if they too are to increase their capacity to respond to market needs.

So how do individuals and organizations change and develop to move with the trends that we find emerging? At a workshop looking at future developments to the National Standard a group of employers and practitioners considered the notion of levels of learning. In Chapter 4, the idea of triple loop learning was introduced. Here that idea is taken further using some of the ideas generated by the workshop participants.

**Levels of learning**

Before looking at what came out of the workshop it is worth considering what we mean by learning. Figure 7.2 shows Kolb's learning cycle. Kolb considered learning to be a circular and perpetual process with four key stages: experience; observation and reflection on that experience; analysis and learning from that reflection; and trying out of new ways of behaving.

Concrete experience can be planned or accidental but both provide an individual with the opportunity to participate in an activity that will provide some learning. According to Kolb, this would be followed by reflective observation where the learners take time to consider the experience and its significance to the way they act and what the experience has taught them about this. Abstract conceptualization of experience is where the learners are able to use the ideas, theories or principles gained from reflection to apply in other situations, the idea being that this conceptualization would lead to applying more successful approaches or behaviours in other situations.

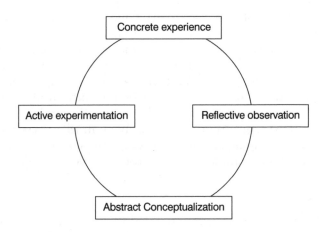

**Figure 7.2** *The learning cycle (based on Kolb et al, 1984)*

Active experimentation would complete the cycle by allowing the learners to try out the learning gained thus far in a variety of situations.

Kolb's theory of learning has led many others to build on the notion of learning, notably Honey and Mumford who designed a questionnaire to help determine learning styles. The questionnaire was designed to help identify how we learn and where our potential weaknesses lie. Learning styles, according to the work of Honey and Mumford, included activists, reflectors, theorists and pragmatists.

Honey and Mumford's work recognized that not everyone will move through each stage of learning at the same pace or indeed with the same ability. This notion was useful since it broke away from the view that learning was a simple progression through a variety of stages. More recently, the idea of levels of learning has been developed. In 1991 Pedler *et al* published a book that showed a framework for a learning company with 11 characteristics that would be found in such an organization. These characteristics ranged from having a learning approach to strategy through to self-development for all. A fundamental aspect of all of this work is the basic assumption that learning is a good thing. More recently, thinking has changed and there is a growing recognition that the real value of learning is where that learning takes us, that is, how we engage with learning to make appropriate decisions to improve our own behaviours and how this can improve our abilities.

**The real value of learning is where it takes us**

Returning then to the workshop that looked at how the National Standard might develop in the future and to how the learning gained by employers and practitioners is moving. Led by Tom Boydell[2], participants considered four levels of learning and how these levels of learning might relate to Investors in People organizations. The idea was that if the process of learning and the direction that new learning might take us could be captured in relation to the National Standard, it might be possible to identify developments for the National Standard that would ensure it remains relevant to organizations in the 21st century. This workshop was the culmination of a year-long process of development activities facilitated by Tom Boydell and Peter Fryer[3] under the guidance of Investors in People UK.

A simple explanation of the four levels of learning is:

Level 0  Doing things anyhow – an ad hoc approach to doing and learning that does not provide an opportunity to reflect or develop.

Level 1  Doing things well – where things are done to an agreed or set standard but are not improved. This approach to learning does not provide for innovation or creativity.

Level 2  Doing things better – where activities are improved and people are involved in the design and implementation of improvements.

Level 3  Doing better things – where a more holistic approach to improving and developing is engendered and individuals take responsibility for their own and others' development.

With the exception of the first level, the remaining three levels provide opportunity for individual and organizational learning and development. Through the application of learning and understanding where each level or mode of learning is appropriate it seems possible that organizations could apply learning principles to build capacity and improve. Using this theory of learning as a basis of discussion the last three levels were applied to the principles of the National Standard. In doing so, the wording of the Standard was considered and an attempt to express the outcomes expected for each principle in terms of learning modes was made. This work was considered alongside the indicators of the National Standard and these were reworded to be expressed in terms of outcomes. The result was a recognition of the need to create a non-judgemental but open-ended approach to the incorporation of the notion of learning into the National Standard.

**Building capacity**

2  Tom Boydell is an academic and writer on learning
3  Peter Fryer is the Chief Executive of Humberside TEC

Figure 7.3, created during the workshop by Steve Burrows[4], captured much of the thinking of the delegates on learning and how learning can help build capacity in organizations. The diagram expresses the idea that for an organization to learn it needs to know which level or mode of learning it is operating and use this knowledge to apply the best level or mode to situations or activities.

The theory is that for learning to be useful it has to be recognized as learning and so an organization needs to be aware or knowledgeable about the types of learning it is applying. By being aware of the different modes of learning an organization can make appropriate choices about the mode it needs to operate to build capacity. Implicit in this notion is the view that all three modes or levels of learning are equally valuable, if applied in the appropriate context. To help clarify this the following example shows how this theory might apply. The case study is based on a real business and the theory has been restated in simple terms after each principle to show how the organization is applying the different levels of learning.

It is clear from the case study that the organization is applying the three levels of learning although, as yet, they have no knowledge of this thinking. Consequently to enable the organization to make appropriate choices, they need to be made aware of the levels linked to Investors in People through the assessment process.

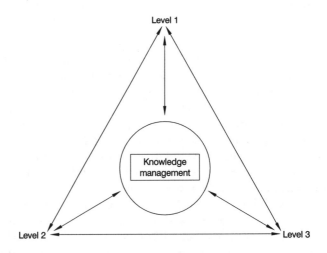

**Figure 7.3** *Knowledge management and levels of learning*

4  Steve Burrows is an Investors in People assessment unit manager

## Lynn Jones Research Limited

Lynn Jones Research Limited is a small market research company based in Edinburgh. Formed in 1998, the company provides a comprehensive research service incorporating planning and project management, project delivery, qualitative and quantitative research, data analysis, questionnaire design and research workshops. The company specializes in tourist-related research for the private and public sectors.

The company was established when all three employees were made redundant from Edinburgh and Lothian's Tourist Board's research department when ELTB was obliged to lose its research department. The company makes use of a number of sub-contractors to conduct part of their fieldwork. Since 1998 the company has established a strong foothold in the market and Lynn Jones chairs the Market Research Society in Scotland. The company complies with the Code of Conduct of the Market Research Society.

As a new business, the company took the decision to use the Investors in People framework to *establish good habits* in relation to their planning and execution of all aspects of the business. All three employees had previous experience of the National Standard from their earlier employment with the Tourist Board and recognized its potential as a sound approach to business development. As a consequence the company has developed a flexible but systematic approach to the organization and management of the business.

The benefits accrued as a result of using the Investors in People framework include:

- clarity of business objectives;
- clear vision for growth and development of employees and the business;
- a solid reputation in the research field;
- development and successful launch of new products, including a major contract with the Greater Glasgow Hotels' Association;
- new business opportunities and growth potential.

## COMMITMENT: THE EVIDENCE

The company has four Values that underpin its approach to development. One of these Values states 'Absolute commitment to company and individual learning'. This Value has clearly been translated into a reality as the company progresses towards becoming a learning organization. All employees were able to articulate this Value and provide clear examples of how they are communicated with and the commitment towards individual and company learning and development. The Staff Handbook sets out the company's three goals. These goals act as the key drivers of the business and are used effectively in the business planning and decision-making process. All employees made unprompted reference to these goals during interviews. Individual contributions to the success of the business are communicated through induction, appraisal and project planning meetings. All employees were able to express with great clarity their individual contribution to the running of the business and how this contributed towards its success.

### Levels of learning/learning modes

*Level 1 Doing things well*
A level 1 approach to commitment would show a 'top down' approach to the development of the organization's direction with little or no input from employees. Ideas for the organization's direction and its goals would be communicated through a downward process of transmission.

*Level 2 Doing things better*
At level 2 communication and organizational direction is a more evolutionary process where employees are actively encouraged to seek out understanding of the vision and add to its effectiveness by inputting their own ideas. There is a more empowered workforce with consultation of a wide range of stakeholders.

*Level 3 Doing better things*
At level 3, there is a deliberate attempt to create mutually worthwhile and purposeful work and this is actively supported through individual learning and participation in the learning of others.

## PLANNING: THE EVIDENCE

The company has a written plan with clearly defined objectives, a Strengths, Weaknesses, Opportunities and Threats (SWOT) analysis and marketing strategy. The plan is reviewed formally every six months by the two directors and the IT manager. In the period between the formal reviews all three employees review specific projects, new opportunities or changes in the marketplace in the marketing update meetings that take place on a monthly basis.

To complement the business plan a separate training and development plan is used to link the business objectives to individual training and development needs. This plan is reviewed at the same time as the business plan and contains details of who is to be trained, in what way, at what time and at what cost. The plan also contains details of the method of delivery and the expected benefits to be gained as a result of the training undertaken.

A formal Performance Review and Development (PRD) process has been in operation since the company was established. This process is aimed at individuals and operates on a six-monthly cycle with additional meetings taking place where new projects identify the need for further development. Where projects highlight the need for team-based development this is noted in the project plan and linked to the PRD process. Training records capture this additional activity. At an organizational level, the review of the company's business objectives acts as an appropriate appraisal of training and development.

Formally, responsibility for training and development rests with the Company Secretary. As the business is small, all employees are active in the pursuit of personal development. The Company Handbook states that '. . . staff are also developed by venturing beyond their comfort zone from time to time.' This attitude towards developing people ensures that responsibility for such activity is firmly embedded in each individual's approach to learning and development.

The company training and development plan links all training and development activity to a specific business objective. Each item of development activity is expressed to show the specific outcomes that are expected to be achieved as a result of the development activity. For example:

| | |
|---|---|
| Business objective: | Learn about financial services products |
| Training need: | To help diversify into that sector |
| Who: | Lynn, Sue |
| How to be met: | Awareness session by the Royal Bank of Scotland to be arranged by the company's business relationship manager |
| Costs: | 1 day |
| By: | May 1999 |
| Outcome/Benefits: | Excellent. Overview of structure and thinking – and gave a lead for a particular business idea. |

This is a typical example of the clarity in establishing business goals linked to training and development and is repeated at individual, team and organizational levels.

Currently the vocational qualifications for market research are suspended pending a review. The company is active in the Market Research Society and makes extensive use of the programme of training offered through this institution.

## Levels of learning/learning modes

### Level 1  Doing things well

At level 1 the focus is to help people learn to do things the 'right' way. The focus is on value for money, meeting targets and meeting customer needs.

### Level 2  Doing things better

Level 2 focuses on making improvements to what already happens. Some consultation about goals and targets take place and there is a higher level of personal satisfaction and development for employees. Individuals are encouraged to think for themselves, to manage quality improvements and to support customers and suppliers in achieving greater satisfaction from improvements made.

### Level 3  Doing better things

At level 3, there is a deliberate attempt to create mutually acceptable goals and targets that are interrelated and involve all stakeholders. There is a greater acknowledgement of differing aspirations and an acceptance that these aspirations should not lead to conflict, but should be used to create opportunity for learning and growth. This notion extends to create matrix management approaches across organizational boundaries and stakeholder groups. Learning is seen as a fundamental aspect of capacity building in individual and organizational terms.

## Action: the evidence

An induction programme has been developed and is used for any temporary employees or sub-contractors. As no new employees have been taken on since the company was established, the induction programme has not been tested for full-time employees. As part of the project management process all employees are introduced effectively to new projects' aims and objectives and how they will contribute to the success of these. Effective procedures are in place and strong evidence of implementation was available to the

Assessor. Appraisals, project review meetings, training plans and training records all reflect that managers are effective in carrying out their responsibilities for training and developing employees.

Training and development activity takes place formally and informally. Line managers, as part of the normal day-to-day operations, carry out a proportion of the training and development activity. Shadowing activities have been highly successful in assisting employees to gain new skills or increased confidence in their own abilities. This approach is supplemented by the formal mechanisms described above.

Training and development opportunities are identified at appraisal meetings and in project review meetings. As a small company many opportunities are identified as a result of day-to-day activity where observations from colleagues point to the need for additional training directly related to their jobs. This ad hoc input supports the more formal approach adopted by the company and adds to the rigour with which training and development activity is identified. Employees were clear that the identification of learning opportunities and training and development needs was a joint responsibility of all involved. Individual training records capture the training and development activity that has taken place. Project review meetings record team-based activity and the business plan captures the broad development needs to progress business objectives. The sum of these three approaches is a clear record of training and development activity against individual, team and organizational needs.

## Levels of learning/learning modes

### Level 1 Doing things well
At level 1 action involves directed learning and development. Individuals are likely to be instructed in 'how to do things well', exercises and simulations and ongoing supervised activity is used to ensure compliance with rules and regulations.

### Level 2 Doing things better
At level 2 activity will involve much more problem solving and participative learning styles. There will be more learning on the job and sharing of good practice with input from individuals to create better ways of working. Piloting of ideas and initiatives, feeding back and adopting better ways of working will all feature in level 2 activity.

*Level 3  Doing better things*

At level 3, there will be greater recognition of individuality for learning modes with acceptance that no one way is best. World issues and broader thinking will feature as the norm. The aspirations and fears of individuals will be accepted as part of normal behaviour. Consensus with all stakeholders will feature as part of the working together principle, which is adopted throughout the organization. A sense of community will develop through the body of shared knowledge aimed at achieving better ways of working and new modes of operation.

## EVALUATION: THE EVIDENCE

The company's approach to the identification of needs and the method of recording this against business objectives provides a strong platform from which the impact of this activity can be measured. All interviewees talked about learning as a normal process of business life. This attitude reflected the approach taken to improve skills and knowledge in order to improve the business operation. Each new project was viewed as a learning opportunity and used to improve skills and behaviours that could then be transferred to other aspects of the company's work. The evaluation of this approach is captured in the business plan reviews, training records and the training and development plans.

The company performance and the performance of individuals are formally recorded in the business plan update meetings and appraisals. Both of these activities take place on a six-monthly cycle. The training and development plan is evaluated throughout the year and updated at the same time as the business plan. Performance measures are established through the objectives-setting procedure and are evaluated on an activity-by-activity basis.

The contribution of training and development to the achievement of goals and targets is evaluated through the processes shown above. There were many examples provided in the portfolio and during interviews, for example:

| | |
|---|---|
| Business objective: | Run Forecaster project |
| Training need: | Awareness and use of Macros |
| Who: | David |
| How to be met: | Tutoring by project analyst |
| Cost: | 1 day |
| Outcome/benefit: | Able to run project successfully. |

This method of recording and evaluating training and development ensures that the contribution of learning is aligned to the achievement of business goals and targets. It also establishes the costs and expected benefits to be gained from the investment made in training and development.

There is a strong belief that only relevant training and development should take place for employees and this translates into a critical view of any activity that may be identified. All interviewees expressed the view that individual learning styles were the key determinant of the identification of the type of training and development activity undertaken. This attitude held the key to how improvements to training and development took place. Critical examination of activity is conducted by all employees and changes made as appropriate. For example, one member of staff attended an open programme on the use of a spreadsheet package (Excel). After reporting back it was decided that in-house training would be more relevant to the company's needs. The IT manager undertook to mentor the individual through the training required.

## Levels of learning/learning modes

### Level 1 Doing things well
At level 1 the evaluation of development will be specific to the activities carried out. No attempt will be made to capture the broader developments that may occur. The emphasis is on what is happening now and not what might occur in the future. Learning that may have occurred and that could facilitate greater capacity for the future will largely be ignored or not recognized. Much of what is evaluated will be captured through summative assessment techniques.

### Level 2 Doing things better
At level 2 evaluation will be more broadly based. Individuals will work together to create opportunity for each other and some non-directional developments will be recognized as valuable contributors to individual growth and organizational capacity building. Formative assessment and acceptance of the need to change will be viewed as the norm. Groups of individuals will act together to seek solutions and share these solutions with others.

### Level 3 Doing better things
At level 3, a body of knowledge will develop whereby improvements

are shared collectively and recognized as worthwhile and valuable. Many solutions will be applied to problems and many individuals will act together to create development opportunities. At this level there will be an acceptance that creative and innovative solutions to problems will occur.

The above case study does not attempt to show which levels of learning are operating in Lynn Jones Research; instead it shows the types of activities and behaviours that might be expected at the different levels of learning. It is clear, however, that Lynn Jones Research is operating at different levels of learning appropriate to their needs at this time. By showing how the levels of learning can be applied, this organization can make informed choices about whether they need to change any of the individual or organizational behaviours either to meet, exceed or create market changes.

## Creating the future

**Rate of change**

Change is often feared yet we deal with change every day of our lives. The fear of change frequently comes from a lack of understanding or willingness to accept that there are very few constants in life. As people have developed throughout the centuries ideas have been adopted to enhance the future and create new opportunity for the ingenuity of mankind to make the most of our surroundings. Processes and technologies progress at a rate of change equal and sometimes in advance of mere mortals' ability to keep up. In this chapter I have tried to express some of the current thinking about developments in the National Standard and the direction it may take in the future. Nothing is certain, except that developments will occur and that the Standard will continue to move to reflect trends in organizational development and individuals' capacity and willingness to change.

# ◀ APPENDIX 1 ▶

# BLANK MATRIX OF WRITTEN EVIDENCE

| Evidence/Reference Number | 1.1 | 1.2 | 1.3 | 1.4 | 2.1 | 2.2 | 2.3 | 2.4 | 2.5 | 2.6 | 2.7 | 3.1 | 3.2 | 3.3 | 3.4 | 3.5 | 3.6 | 4.1 | 4.2 | 4.3 | 4.4 | 4.5 | 4.6 |
|---|---|---|---|---|---|---|---|---|---|---|---|---|---|---|---|---|---|---|---|---|---|---|---|
| | | | | | | | | | | | | | | | | | | | | | | | |
| | | | | | | | | | | | | | | | | | | | | | | | |
| | | | | | | | | | | | | | | | | | | | | | | | |
| | | | | | | | | | | | | | | | | | | | | | | | |
| | | | | | | | | | | | | | | | | | | | | | | | |
| | | | | | | | | | | | | | | | | | | | | | | | |
| | | | | | | | | | | | | | | | | | | | | | | | |
| | | | | | | | | | | | | | | | | | | | | | | | |
| | | | | | | | | | | | | | | | | | | | | | | | |

**Figure A1.1** *Blank evidence matrix*

# ◀ APPENDIX 2 ▶
# THE NATIONAL STANDARD

## Investors in People: The four principles and indicators

The four principles of the Investors in People National Standard have been broken down into 23 indicators, which are the basis for assessment.

### Principle One: Commitment

> An Investor in People makes a commitment from the top to develop all employees to achieve business objectives.

1.1 The commitment from top management to train and develop employees is communicated effectively throughout the organization.

1.2 Employees at all levels are aware of the broad aims or vision of the organization.

1.3 The organization has considered what employees at all levels will contribute to the success of the organization, and has communicated this effectively to them.

1.4 Where representative structures exist, communication takes place between management and representatives on the vision of where the organization is going and the contribution that employees (and their representatives) will make to its success.

### Principle Two: Planning

> An Investor in People reviews the needs and plans the training and development of all employees.

2.1 A written but flexible plan sets out the organization's goals and targets.

2.2 A written plan identifies the organization's training and development needs, and specifies what actions will be taken to meet these needs.

2.3 Training and development needs are regularly reviewed against goals and targets at the organization, team and individual level.

2.4 A written plan identifies the resources that will be used to meet training and development needs.

2.5 Responsibility for training and developing employees is clearly identified and understood throughout the organization, starting at the top.

2.6 Objectives are set for training and development actions at the organization, team and individual level.

2.7 Where appropriate, training and development targets are linked to external standards, and particularly to National Vocational Qualifications (NVQs) or Scottish Vocational Qualifications (SVQs) and units.

## Principle Three: Action

An Investor in People takes action to train and develop individuals on recruitment and throughout their employment.

3.1 All new employees are introduced effectively to the organization and all employees new to a job are given the training and development they need to do that job.

3.2 Managers are effective in carrying out their responsibilities for training and developing employees.

3.3 Managers are actively involved in supporting employees to meet their training and development needs.

3.4 All employees are made aware of the training and development opportunities open to them.

3.5 All employees are encouraged to help identify and meet their job-related development needs.

3.6 Action takes place to meet the training and development needs of individuals, teams and the organization.

## Principle Four: Evaluation

An Investor in People evaluates the investment in training and development to assess achievement and improve future effectiveness.

4.1 The organization evaluates the impact of training and development actions on knowledge, skills and attitude.

4.2 The organization evaluates the impact of training and development actions on performance.

4.3 The organization evaluates the contribution of training and development to the achievement of its goals and targets.

4.4 Top management understand the broad cost and benefit of training and developing employees.

4.5   Action takes place to implement improvements to training and development identified as a result of evaluation.

4.6   Top management's continuing commitment to training and developing employees is demonstrated to all employees.

# ◀ APPENDIX 3 ▶

# REVISED INDICATORS: READY RECKONER

| Existing indicator | Revised indicator | Existing indicator | Revised indicator |
|---|---|---|---|
| 1.1 | 1.1 | 3.1 | 3.1 |
| 1.2 | 1.2 | 3.2 | 3.6 |
| 1.3 | 2.1 | 3.3 | 3.4 |
| 1.4 | 2.2 | 3.4 | 3.5 |
| 1.5 | 1.3 | 3.5 | 3.6 |
| 1.6 | 1.4 | 3.6 | 3.3 |
| 2.1 | 2.4 | 4.1 | 4.3 |
| 2.2 | 2.3 | 4.2 | 4.1 |
| 2.3 | 2.3 | 4.3 | 4.2 |
| 2.4 | 2.5 | 4.4 | 4.4 |
| 2.5 | 3.2 | 4.5 | 4.6 |
| 2.6 | 2.6 | 4.6 | 4.5 |
| 2.7 | 2.7 | | |

# USEFUL CONTACT ADDRESSES

Investors in People UK
7–10 Chandos Street
London W1M 9DE
http://www.iipuk.co.uk

British Quality Foundation
32–34 Great Peter Street
London SW1P 2QX
http://www.quality-
foundation.co.uk

Quality Scotland Foundation
13 Abercromby Place
Edinburgh EH3 6LB
http://www.qualityscotland.co.uk

Investors in People Scotland
13 Abercromby Place
Edinburgh EH3 6LB

European Foundation for
Quality Management
Brussels Representative Office
Avenue des Pleiades 15
1200 Brussels
Belgium
http://www.efqm.org

Scottish Qualifications Authority
Hanover House
24 Douglas Street
Glasgow G2 7NQ
http://www.sqa.org.uk

# INDEX